The 3 Simple Secrets of Success after the Diploma

Also by Janis Dietz

Yes, You Can: Go Beyond Physical Adversity and Live Life to Its Fullest.
New York: Demos Medical Publishing
1-888799-48-X

The 3 Simple Secrets of Success after the Diploma

Integrity, Persistence, and Discipline

Janis Dietz, Ph.D

iUniverse, Inc.
New York Lincoln Shanghai

The 3 Simple Secrets of Success after the Diploma
Integrity, Persistence, and Discipline

iUniverse books may be ordered through booksellers or by contacting:

iUniverse
2021 Pine Lake Road, Suite 100
Lincoln, NE 68512
www.iuniverse.com
1-800-Authors (1-800-288-4677)

Cover Art by MALKI

ISBN: 978-0-595-46926-0 (pbk)
ISBN: 978-0-595-91211-7 (ebk)

Printed in the United States of America

To my students, who face great challenges and great opportunities.

I learn from you every day and your potential continues to delight me.

The true importance of integrity, persistence, and discipline:

Nothing great or lasting in the world has been accomplished without them.

Contents

Acknowledgments

This journey has been a multiyear process. Many people were helpful during the process.

My thanks go to:

- First, my students. As a second career, teaching has been a rewarding lesson in process and technique for reaching a very diverse customer base. My students have taught me, listened to me, told me when they were motivated and when they weren't. They have made me proud of them and given me great joy.
- My parents, Al and Joan Weinstein, who modeled the importance of integrity, persistence, and discipline better than anyone I know.
- Mona Marshall, MALKI, who drew the cover art, loves the theme as she loves teaching, and worked through countless re-formatting of the title and the cover.
- Deborah Mandabach, who provided excellent advice on many of the areas where I struggled.
- Laurie Magers, Zig Ziglar's Executive Assistant, who spent many hours in careful editing. Zig Ziglar has been an incredible mentor to me and his entire staff has given me hope for my message.
- The faculty and Dean of the College of Business and Public Management at The University of La Verne, who listened to my ideas and were wonderful supporters of this non-academic project; and to the Faculty Professional Support Committee for their financial support.
- Of course, mostly to my husband, John. He, most of all, suffered through the writing, the expense, and the frustration that every author

endures. He is my true partner and I would have crumbled without him. I wish for all of my students a partner like him.

Preface

As you Graduate ... the World is yours to Conquer—go out and Conquer it!

Congratulations, graduate. You are about to learn that you don't pay the price for success, you enjoy it. You actually pay the price for failure; you pay the price for not taking advantage of all the riches now before you. You are living at the best possible time in the best possible country and the world stands before you for conquering. Fasten your seatbelts and get ready to enjoy the ride! After you have finished this book, you will recognize what you need to do to be as successful as you want to be and you will be ready for the challenges and opportunities before you. Relax; you don't even have to take notes!

I am fortunate to have enjoyed two careers. For seventeen years, I held sales and sales management jobs in the hardware/home center industry, calling on customers such as Home Depot and Lowe's. I learned a lot about the importance and the cost of integrity, persistence and discipline in those jobs. As a college professor for the past eleven years, I have enjoyed and continue to enjoy, the chance to teach my students the principles learned in that long career; principles that I have been encouraged to share with you here.

As a twenty-four year veteran of the corporate minefields and an eleven year veteran of the classroom minefields, I speak from two perspectives. One is the world into which most of you will go, earning a living working at or owning a for-profit or non-profit company. They both essentially require the same skills (I have worked for both). The other is the world from which you are about to depart, that classroom you could not wait to leave. I know it will be tough. I know that about a year from now you will realize why your professors wanted you to come to class on time, why some used "tough love" more than coddling, why people like me would not let you wear baseball caps or "iM" each other in the classroom. Maybe it won't take a year, but it will happen. You will realize why we made you take biology, and history, and English. When your children come to you for help with their homework, you will be glad you took those courses. When your employees need counseling and direction, that psychology course will come to your mind. As our natural resource challenges become greater, you will have a better understanding of them because you took science. Everything makes you smarter. Though technology has already made many of your skills outdated, you have the tools to learn new ones. A college degree teaches you to know where to find information; it gives you the skills to learn even more valuable information. It proves you know how to set and achieve a difficult goal. It is the true beginning of your fabulous life. But you must never stop learning because the rewards for learning will increase in direct proportion to your effort. Plus, as an added benefit, continuous mental activity can help prevent Alzheimer's disease!

As Admiral William Halsey said, *"There aren't any great men. There are just great challenges that ordinary men like you and me are forced by circumstances to meet."* This will become clear throughout the book as I urge you to make choices and respond to challenges with integrity, persistence and discipline in mind.

Why did I pick integrity, persistence, and discipline?

- I picked integrity because, as a salesman (the word man is generic for human being), it has always been the most prized part of my "brand" (see Chapter 11). Once you lose your integrity, the walls start to crumble on everything.

- I picked persistence because it is responsible for more than 90 percent of success. I think it was Woody Allen who said "90 percent is just showing up." You must have integrity at the starting gate, but persistence keeps you on course and eventually leads you to your goal.

- I picked discipline because integrity and persistence have to be organized! You must have the discipline to focus on the most important things first, the discipline to say no to activities that do not contribute to your goals, and the discipline to use wisely the same twenty-four hours a day that everyone else possesses.

This book contains twenty chapters, weaving the theme of integrity, persistence, and discipline throughout. There is a discussion about learning from all sources, appreciating the fact that the world is changing and requires new skills to succeed, and the importance of networking as those changes occur. In terms of the mistakes that you will invariably make, using them as a learning occasion will become clear, as well as the opportunities those mistakes afford you and the indisputable need to take responsibility for them quickly and honestly. Changing your mindset from the grade to the opportunity is important and you will learn about the importance of translating all you learned plus your passion into goals that stretch your perspective. In the end, you will know that you can't give up on your goals, that you must believe in yourself to succeed, and that failure is a welcomed event on the way to success.

My purpose here is to send you on your way with excitement about what you bring to your new life, and some suggestions of tools that can help you make the most of the rest of that life. Life is not a dress rehearsal. Every day is a chance to contribute, to our world, to your family and to yourself. Make the most of every one of those days. Never look back; always look forward. Abraham Lincoln said, *"You will be about as happy as you make up your mind to be."* Your attitude is more important than your aptitude, as my friend Zig Ziglar reminds his audiences.

Remember these words: Integrity, Persistence, and Discipline. You will require all of them to meet your goals and you will need to remember them to keep you on track. Before you delve into the rest of the book, say the words out loud:

Integrity, persistence, and discipline

Let me close this preface by sharing the words of the late Dr. Peter Drucker, the most widely read management writer in the world:

"We live in an age of unprecedented opportunity: If you've got ambition and smarts, you can rise to the top of your chosen profession, regardless of where you started out." [1]

1

Learn from Each Other

The world is and will become more diverse. You will be working and playing with people who come from different ethnic backgrounds, different religions, and different countries. We know from research that companies are more productive with a diverse workforce. Your generation is used to diversity and I am here to tell you that it will make your life vastly more rewarding, as it has mine.

There is evidence that members of different racial and ethnic groups tend to prefer socializing with members of their own groups. You can help to change that. You can help us get to a colorless and seamless society, you more than any other generation in history. You are perfect for this task because you recognize that your generation is more alike than you are different. If you stand next to someone from another country or another race, you will agree that you both want love, acceptance, and accomplishment. You will be able to teach your children to welcome people of other races and origins, not to shun them. Prejudice is taught, and you can avoid teaching it to your children and practicing it in the workplace. As a generation, you can make progress in what has taken thousands of years and cost millions of lives to eradicate. What a great contribution! Are you with me so far?

Learn from the different perspectives of your colleagues because each of you comes from different "schemas." After all, we have more than two political parties (sometimes, more than three) in the United States. Their differences help to make our country better. The last thing you want is to be a victim of "group think," where everyone touts the same party line. There must be analysis, debate, and disagreement. You will learn why your colleagues feel strongly about something and you will learn to appreciate the growth opportunities for you in understanding them. I have recently developed a seminar for our university focusing on students who are the first generation in their family to attend college. I learned so much about the different backgrounds and orientations from which first-generation students come, and how to help them succeed. *"Seek first to understand"* is a good way to go about the business of living.

In your career, you will work with people much older than you, who have not grown up with the technological savvy you have (remember, not all of us grew up with computers, fax machines and microwave ovens). They will learn from you ways to make whatever business you are in better because you have the energy and the skills to do that. You will learn from them skills that work in helping you to do your job better because their experience gives them some talents that will benefit you. Celebrate what you can learn from each other! But also celebrate that you have so much to learn about life. I had a freshman in the class I just spoke about who was convinced that he knew everything about the world and that it was bad. After four months, I saw him start to change his mind after being exposed to other ideas. As each semester has passed, he has changed his views a little bit as the courses he studies have helped him broaden his learning community. I expect to continue to see that growth as he nears graduation.

Business in the future will require multinational teams to accomplish tasks in just about every industry. Companies like IBM are putting together teams of people from all over the world and using technology to solve problems for many of their customers. There will be many opportunities for you to use teamwork to broaden your skills and achieve recognition.

Another area that is evolving is the need for leadership skills. MBA programs have long focused on quantitative and strategic skills, sometimes leaving graduates without the "soft" skills so in need in a business world with fewer layers of management than in previous years. Recently, recruiters told professors at MIT that graduates needed better leadership skills.[2] Many schools are embracing the need to change educational offerings as world challenges dictate. "Learning from each other" and being open to learning more ways to communicate with each other will continue to be a topic of corporate training priorities.

Change is hard. Be open to changes that will come in your life as technology and population movements force changes in the world. By learning from each other, you can make those changes easier to embrace. When the Euro was first introduced in Europe in 1999 as a way to reduce the complication of traveling from country to country, there was confusion. It has proven to be a good thing, albeit a change that required adaptation. The added security at airports since 9/11 has been a boon to the slip-on shoe industry and a hardship for bottled water concessions, but we have adapted. The most incredible inventions and business opportunities have come from the need to adapt to change. If you look at the number of people telecommuting now, at least ten percent of the workforce, you can see that the need to adapt to long commutes and crowded metropolitan areas has opened opportunities in a number of industries. There will be many changes like this in your life. You will probably see the end of paper checks, VCR machines, perhaps even gasoline. With each change, you will grow. And because your minds are wired to absorb all that new stuff, you will be able to help the next generation continue to make the world a better place.

Integrity, persistence, and discipline—do these fit here?

2

Find something You are Passionate About

I often rave in class about some of my former employers, including General Electric, Johnson & Johnson, and Delta Faucet. Some students think I am crazy, but I truly love those companies. I have been fortunate in my life to work for companies about whose mission I am passionate. Notice I said mission and not product. Many of the products I have sold, including extension cords and toilets, are not glamorous, but the mission to take care of customers and employees is something that I could be proud of and passionate about every day. Some of you will be forced to take jobs that are not what you know you want forever. Don't feel alone. Very few people either know what they want or have the opportunity to pursue it early in their careers. Be patient. It is worth waiting and exploring the many options out there. But know, in your heart, that persistence, integrity, and discipline will get you wherever you want to go, eventually. Every time you doubt yourself, remember those words.

Employee engagement, the extent to which workers are committed to their organizations, improves performance and retention.[3] If you find a cause or business that you truly love, you will be happier, more productive, and less likely to leave. But if you take a job that promises a big salary but does not excite you beyond the paycheck, you will eventually regret it. It is a tremendous boost to your peace of mind to work for a company that treats its people well, that creates products or services that are good for society, and that affords you the chance to grow and learn every day. The best companies to work for often have lower employee turnover and, in turn, higher stock prices for their investors. Under that scenario, everyone benefits.

If you don't chase money, but chase the excitement that comes when you are committed and passionate about something, money will inevitably follow. It might take a few years, but it is a surer way to happiness. I have countless stories of students who graduated and took the "next sure thing," only to come back within a year searching for something that could give them meaning. You have probably heard the phrase coined by famous football coach, Vince Lombardi, *"Winning is the only thing."* Well, I don't quite agree with Coach Lombardi because I think losing has a lot to teach us. In the last century, as the baby boomers hit their stride, winning and making lots of money were very important and a measure of the person. But, that left behind lots of marriages, missed children's activities, and family opportunities never to be made up. Enter the 21st century—the emphasis is now on winning at the whole package life has to offer, and not necessarily at the expense of others.[4] Flatter organizations, those with less vertical levels of management, have opened more opportunities for performance to be rewarded. So you don't have to chase money. There are plenty of opportunities and there is plenty of time to explore career choices.

I am always hesitant to use the word "passion" among my eighteen- to twenty-two-year-old students, but you are more mature now. You know (hopefully) that a relationship takes a lot of work, but that it is worth the effort. Anything I have done in my life pales in comparison to my marriage of twenty-six years. Relationships with customers and co-workers tend to outlast jobs and even industries. I remember working on the results of a survey I did for my Ph.D. dissertation. I surveyed 248 executive MBA graduates from four western universities. The average age was thirty-seven. What do these people remember and value most about their MBA experience? They value team members and study groups. With the rise in on-line MBA programs, I am continually reminded that it is the relationships between human beings, both romantic and in friendships, which truly give us meaning in our lives. To be passionate about doing the right things for people and customers is at the heart of successful businesses.

I have sold everything from disposable diapers to wire and cable in my life. What made me passionate about these decidedly dull products? The people, the way we were treated by our employer, the pride that everyone took in taking care of customers enabled me to be passionate about these employers. I once drove to Los Angeles International Airport to pick up a reel of GE wire that Fender Rhodes Guitar Company needed to get their production line going. Knowing that many people would benefit from that action made it easy to see excitement in wire as well as to get on the freeway at 4 am!

I will give you an example of why it is easy for me to be passionate about Johnson & Johnson. In 1979, cyanide-laced Tylenol® tablets in Chicago killed five people. Now think for a minute about J&J's options: The deaths were limited to Chicago, so Johnson & Johnson had no requirement to take back product from anywhere but Chicago. They had another option, to take back all Tylenol® products across the country, at a cost of about $200 million and perhaps the end of their brand. Before you decide what they should have done, here is J&J's credo, the one in operation when I worked for them and the one in operation today:

Johnson & Johnson

Our Credo[5]

We believe our first responsibility is to the doctors, nurses and patients,
to mothers and fathers and all others who use our products and services.
In meeting their needs everything we do must be of high quality.
We must constantly strive to reduce our costs
in order to maintain reasonable prices.
Customers' orders must be serviced promptly and accurately.
Our suppliers and distributors must have an opportunity
to make a fair profit.

We are responsible to our employees,
the men and women who work with us throughout the world.
Everyone must be considered as an individual.
We must respect their dignity and recognize their merit.
They must have a sense of security in their jobs.
Compensation must be fair and adequate,
and working conditions clean, orderly and safe.
We must be mindful of ways to help our employees fulfill
their family responsibilities.
Employees must feel free to make suggestions and complaints.
There must be equal opportunity for employment, development
and advancement for those qualified.
We must provide competent management,
and their actions must be just and ethical.
We are responsible to the communities in which we live and work
and to the world community as well.
We must be good citizens—support good works and charities
and bear our fair share of taxes.
We must encourage civic improvements and better health and education.
We must maintain in good order
the property we are privileged to Use,
protecting the environment and natural resources.
Our final responsibility is to our stockholders.
Business must make a sound profit.
We must experiment with new ideas.
Research must be carried on, innovative programs developed
and mistakes paid for.
New equipment must be purchased, new facilities provided
and new products launched.
Reserves must be created to provide for adverse times.

When we operate according to these principles,
the stockholders should realize a fair return.

Doesn't that Credo tell it all? Johnson & Johnson did, indeed, take back the entire product around the country; it did indeed cost them $200 million, but they kept their integrity and they kept their customers. I am just as passionate about Johnson & Johnson today as when I worked for them thirty years ago. This also means that I am willing to spend more on their products. Companies like Johnson & Johnson command more customer loyalty and, in turn, reward their stockholders and employees.

Don Shula, the legendary coach of the Miami Dolphins, says that the problem with most leaders is that they don't stand for anything—they are not "conviction driven." *"Leadership implies movement toward something, and convictions provide that direction. If you don't stand for something, you'll fall for anything."*[6] Whether you are reading about football, baseball, or basketball (or hockey or soccer), you know that these players share a passion for and a commitment to what they are doing.

One man who is passionate about football can't even kick one. Doug Blevins is one of football's most revered kicking coaches. At the 2005 Super Bowl, between the Philadelphia Eagles and the New England Patriots, Blevins had players he had coached on both sides, so he couldn't lose. Blevins, who suffers from cerebral palsy, grew up passionate about football. He watched and dissected games, finding a niche as a kicking coach. According to one of his clients, "he's a middle linebacker in a handicapped body."[7] Along with Blevin's passion obviously comes persistence. He figured out what he was passionate about and proceeded to obtain the skills needed to make it happen. He did not chase money. He chased a dream and he made it happen.

Another excellent example of a life passion is George Washing Carver, who invented hundreds of ways to use peanuts and sweet potatoes, and who worked tirelessly to teach farmers how to increase their crop yield. George Washington Carver was born a slave in 1864 but spent most of his career at what is now Tuskegee University in Alabama, where the George Washington Carver Museum stands. Carver never sought patents for his inventions and he never profited from what truly changed the world. He was passionate about flowers and planting.[8] Studying George Washington Carver is a task well worth the effort.

Many of you may love dogs, but how many of you are passionate about leading up to eighteen dogs through 1200 miles of ice and snow? No? I didn't think so. But Libby Riddles is really passionate about dogs! She was the first woman to win the Iditarod, the famous marathon dogsled race from Anchorage to Nome, Alaska, in 1985. Just give some thought to what this entails. It involves feeding, doctoring, transporting food, making "booties" to keep ice from between the dogs' paws, keeping the dogs from being distracted, loving them—and doing it again and again for 1200 miles![9] This is a remarkable story of passion and commitment. You will find that about something in your career, but don't expect to find it today or even tomorrow.

Enterprise Rent-a-Car, the largest rental car company in North America, is guided by their passion and guiding philosophy: "Take care of your customers first … and profits will follow." Their brand, they feel, is *"the most valuable thing we own."*[10] The feedback I get from students who have been recruited by Enterprise is that the company lives this passion and the values that go with it, such as *"Personal honesty and integrity are the foundation of our success"* and *"Customer service is our way of life."*

The late Sam Walton, the founder of Wal-Mart, knew he wanted to go into retailing while he served in the United States Army. He also knew he wanted to go into business for himself. He read extensively about retailing. This is important because the more you know about an area, the more you know about whether it can really be your passion. Sam Walton, who built the world's largest retail business, did not become a billionaire because he was smart, although he was. He was passionate about the retailing business and convinced that he could learn enough to be successful in it[11]. He had lots of obstacles on his way to success. He forgot to add a renewable clause to his first lease on a store in Newport, Arkansas. His success with the store only prompted the owner to refuse to renew the lease, in order to collect more of the tremendous profits Walton had been able to produce in the store. But Sam Walton was passionate about this business and went on to eventually put the Newport store out of business. At this writing, Wal-Mart is the world's largest company, but Sam Walton got there through passion, persistence and through motivating his employees with integrity and discipline.

Entertainer Barry Manilow is somewhat before your time, but he is a great heartthrob for my generation (and for me, in particular). During my adult years, he has always been famous and rich. But he grew up a poor Jewish kid in Brooklyn, New York, just like my father. He started as a mail delivery clerk at CBS. When he realized that music was his passion, he gave it everything he had, studying music at night and playing the piano in clubs on weekends. When he was offered a job in Indiana, he told his CBS boss that he couldn't go because he did not want to forego the security of his CBS job. His boss told him to pursue his passion, but that he would always have a job at CBS if he needed one[12]. That experience makes two of my points: 1) If you are dedicated and responsible at your job (discipline), you will be welcomed back, and, 2) Follow your passion with persistence once you have identified it.

Many of you are football fans and some of you played football in college. So did Jerome Bettis (Notre Dame), but he is not being celebrated as much for that (a Super Bowl championship) as for the Jerome Bettis *The Bus Stops Here Foundation*, which has sent more than 5,000 inner city kids to JB Football Camp in Detroit, has awarded college scholarships, and has built or renovated playgrounds[13]. Bettis has used his fame and money to pursue his real passion, helping kids. Long after other football greats take the spotlight, Bettis' good deeds will be making a difference.

Money comes eventually when a passion like that is followed. Not right away, most of the time, but it does. Besides, the side benefit of doing something you truly love can sustain you while you are building your fortune. One of my former students, Kapono Kobylanski, used to disagree with me about lots of things, but we settled into friendly discussions and he settled into learning why his opinions were not always correct. The following email, received one year after he graduated, delighted me:

> *"Thank you! I wanted to say that first because I am so thankful for my education and experiences at ULV. You have definitely made an impact on my amazing education and experiences. So here's the update with me. After searching and interviewing almost everywhere, I landed my job that I was always dreaming of. I did not know exactly what I wanted in a job, but this job (is) definitely explaining to me what I wanted. As you share this letter or parts of this letter with your current students, tell them that I said: Anything you dream or want can be reality if you put your mind to it, give it your all at all times (HARD WORK), utilize resources that can help you and never lose sight of your goal. The sky is the limit; the only question is what is your limit?"*
>
> *—Kopono Kobylanski*

Now, to be honest with you, Kopono was always passionate! But he has found a job where he can focus that passion. You will, too.

"To love what you do and feel that it matters—how could anything be more fun?

—Katherine Graham

3

Give Your Employer More ...

That's right. If they pay you $50,000, give them $55,000 worth of work, or more. Don't be a clock-watcher, counting the minutes until you can go home. Although it might not seem like it at times, you will be noticed. I have never had to ask for a raise. I always tell students at the beginning of class that I will give them more than they are paying for and they groan. Well, when I get letters from students years after graduation telling me what an impact I had on them, I know it was worth the pain of "getting more than the price you were paying." I got a wonderful letter this Christmas from a graduating senior:

> *"Janis,*
>
> *In my years at The University of La Verne, I was fortunate enough to have met an individual that's so important and vital in my life and career. I am ever so thankful to have learned so much from you and your experiences. I just wanted you to know that I will forever be in debt to you because I feel that I got more than what I paid for with my tuition."*
>
> *Duke Trinh*

You can well imagine my feelings when I read that card. That is why I am here and Duke's card validates my goals to "give the customer more." Another student sent me a frame with collectible stamps in it as a thank you (breaking my policy of no gifts). One of the stamps is 3 cents, released in honor of Labor Day in 1956. The student's comment: "Put in the work and you will be rewarded." This has been an online class and many of the students thought they could skate through it. This particular student is constantly emailing me how amazed he is that his classmates don't want to do their best. In the long run, the rewards they reap will match the effort they put into the process.

In reality, the "cream of the crop" is very small. For instance, if you read one book a month, you are in the top one percent of people in the world. My students always ask about extra credit, but those who embrace their education and do more than expected never have to worry about extra credit (see stamp guy above—he got the highest grade in the class). However, if you are one of those who really did not put in a stellar performance in college (or, like the love of my life, flunked out of junior college twice), take heart. It is never too late to change. It is never too late for that light bulb to go on! By the way, my husband John has enjoyed a very successful career in the grocery industry, despite his inauspicious start. I am always delighted to see seniors who have struggled throughout their four years, and then they get it. They are energized by a new electricity. And everything is worth it, all the nagging, all the pleading, and my frustration. I have learned the hard way that you cannot motivate students until they motivate themselves. To the chagrin of many of my former students, I never seem to stop trying!

I am a big fan of Zig Ziglar, the author of *See You at the Top* and many other best selling books. Zig actually took the time to endorse my first book, *Yes, You Can: Go Beyond Physical Adversity and Live Life to its Fullest.* Much of Zig's success has been because he went above and beyond what was expected by his employer. As he says, *"We seldom, if ever, hear of a person who makes it big only by doing what he is paid to do".*[14] He credits his mother, widowed when he was five years old and with twelve children to rear, with instilling in him responsibility with these words: "When you work for someone, work for them all the way." Sadly, workplace studies show that many workers feel that they are capable of doing 50 percent more work, but don't because of a lack of reward, opportunity (in their mind) for advancement, inadequate training and feeling cut off from decision making[15]. These are self-fulfilling prophecies, aren't they? If these people started to put in the effort, it is very likely that what they feel holds them back would disappear. They have an "external locus of control"; they think that what happens to them is controlled externally. People with an "internal locus of control" know that their efforts or lack of them are responsible for their success. You really want to be around people with an internal locus of control because they are most likely to be on the productive side and contribute to the results of every team in which they participate.

If you put in just five extra minutes each day, that's almost half an hour a week. If you make one extra call a week in sales, that is fifty-two extra calls a year. Let's just say you are in sales and you usually "close" or sell, 10 percent of your calls. If you make ten calls a week, you close one of them. But if you make fifty-two extra calls a year, that's five extra sales! By visualizing how easy it is to produce more and, at the same time, providing your employer with more than he/she expects, everyone wins!

Let's assume that you don't go into sales. Let's assume you become a CPA. What could you do with an extra fifteen minutes a day? That is more than an hour a week of productivity. When you break it into small increments, it becomes easier. It is not hard to go above and beyond what is expected of you and the rewards are great.

Clock-watchers rarely succeed at anything. I have worked with and managed enough of them to know. When I first went to work for General Electric, the other salesman would close his briefcase at 4:45 and wait for the clock to strike 5:00 so he could leave. He eventually left all right, not by his choice. Clock watchers are not there for their employer; they are there for themselves. You and your employer will benefit from an attitude of commitment and getting the job done without regard to what the clock shows.

The American War of Independence effectively ended in 1781. Even though "*it became clear that American Independence was assured, Washington kept drilling the Continental Army to new levels of military discipline just in case the diplomatic efforts collapsed and war resumed.*"[16] George Washington, who could not pay or even provide adequate clothing for his soldiers, motivated them and himself to perform heroic acts almost not humanly possible. There was a greater cause to serve. You have a greater cause to serve as well, one only loosely connected to your paycheck.

As I was preparing to send this book to the publisher, we stayed in a fairly new Hilton Hotel in Branson, Missouri. There was a sign in the business center that they had pre-paid Internet cards. No one at the front desk knew anything about that, even though Hilton themselves is advertising it. I was not happy, but I trudged up to my room to get a credit card because the front desk would not take cash for the prepaid cards that their business center advertised. The next day, I got a note from a valet, Steven Cooper. He had taken the time to find out why Hilton could not answer their customers' questions about a service they were advertising. Was it the job of Steven Cooper to find out and follow-through on this problem? No, but he did, and in the process was able to find the answers, teach the front desk personnel how to sell the cards, and make me happy as well! He went above and beyond his job description and I have no doubt he will go far with Hilton!

Zig Ziglar loves to tell the story of Dave Anderson, who was working for the railroad on a hot day, when he was summoned by the president of the railroad, Jim Murphy, from his private car. The two men spent about an hour together and Dave returned to the crew, who wanted to know how Dave knew the president of the railroad and, if he did, why "he was still working in the hot sun and Jim Murphy had gotten to be President." Dave explained, "It is very simple. We went to work for the railroad on the same day. Twenty-three years ago, I went to work for $1.75 an hour and Jim Murphy went to work for the railroad."[17]

Go to work for the railroad. You will never look back.

Another way to put this concept is "under-promise" and "over-deliver." It may seem strange not to promise an employer or prospective partner everything you think you can do, but the effect of "getting more than you are paying for" is delight in the customer's mind and long-term loyalty that can't as easily be upset by the competition (or person competing). Take Amazon.com, the online merchant. They consistently under promise and over deliver. They usually ship books I order within twenty-four hours, even if they have promised three to five working days. I am a raving fan of Amazon.com, even though I pass Borders and Barnes & Noble almost daily. Are the books any different? No, but I am buying more than books. I am buying a long-term relationship. In sales, we know that customers don't care how much you know until they know how much you care. I have never met anyone from Amazon.com, but I think they care and they certainly give me more than I am paying for in communication and service for what may be a hard to differentiate product.

Actually, businesses become successful with just this simple strategy. Sam Walton told his team to *"Go all-out to exceed customers' expectations and make sure that customers have a good time shopping at Wal-Mart."*[18] By looking at your responsibility as a "product" selling your services to an employer, you can see how giving beyond expectations pays off for everyone.

I recently followed up on some research I did a few years ago, where I asked employers all across the country what kinds of jobs they were offering to college graduates. Along the way I asked about problems they have with newly hired college graduates. Do you know what topped their list?"

1. "Work ethic"

2. "Flexibility"

3. "Not expecting to always be able to leave at five"

These are the same comments I heard two years ago, so my conclusion is that young college graduates who give their best to their employers and show initiative have wonderful career opportunities, regardless of their college major. I have found in my career that there are so few people who really meet these criteria that employers are surprised and delighted when they find such an employee.

Discipline is required to sell fish, don't you think? The best seller *Fish!*[19] was inspired by the Pike Place Market in Seattle, where happy employees commune and laugh with customers as they send fish flying through the air. In an era when a high percentage of employees are not happy, the book describes the secret to success with customers:

1. Choose your attitude. Every day, you choose your attitude toward your customers and your employer. It is not chosen for you.

2. Be present. Cell phones and instant messaging systems cause "noise" that often blocks out listening to and responding to customers. The person (employer or customer) you are with is the most important person at that time. It is good marriage advice as well!

3. Play! Life is too short not to enjoy your surroundings. Pick employers who "play" once in awhile.

4. Make their day. I once had a woman at McDonalds serve me with such cheer that it "made my day". Yesterday I was at Starbucks waiting to talk to the manager about a charitable donation. Just watching the young woman who was serving customers made my day! She was so cheerful that you could not leave there in a bad mood! And by the way, I make it a point to advise the managers of these exemplary employees of my excellent experience.

You can see that the point here is to give your customers and your employer more than the price of your services. The rewards will come back many times.

Integrity, Persistence and Discipline

4

Welcome Responsibility for Mistakes—it is Cheaper

Let's suppose you hit someone's bumper in the parking lot. No one sees you. Why is it cheaper to leave them a note rather than just to leave?

1. Integrity is what happens when no one is looking. It is one of, if not the most, important trait of leaders. It is the most important for me and for the most ethical of salespeople. Leaving the note shows integrity.

2. If you don't admit the mistake, you will remember it and always worry that someone will find out. There is a cost to worry.

3. The bumper will have to be fixed and the other person or his/her insurance company will have to pay for it. You will know that.

I am amazed and saddened for you when I see public figures admit fraud or marital indiscretions only after they know they have been found out. If they had admitted their mistakes at the beginning, the public would have forgiven them (maybe), but they make it worse by denying their actions until they have no choice. Lies and cover-ups only make the price higher in the end. There is no doubt that you can't get away with it because there are no secrets anymore. President Bill Clinton found this out, Martha Stewart found this out, and the late Ken Lay, of Enron, found this out. As smart as these people are or were, they paid a price for something that should have been so easy for a leader of their talents, admitting mistakes.

Last year the church in my hometown, which was founded some sixty plus years ago, was truly let down by a trusted minister who admitted to plagiarizing thirty-four sermons, only after he was discovered to have done so. To my father, a long-time member and former Chairman of the Board, this was the best minister they have ever hired. Yet the Board of Trustees had no choice but to fire him. His excuse was that he thought he was not good enough. For this feeble excuse, his career as a minister is over, he has let down people who adored him, and he will have caused an irreparable rift in a wonderful and loving group of people who have given generously to provide him with a pulpit to call his own. There were many ways that this tragedy could have been avoided if he had just come forth from the very beginning.

You also learn more from mistakes than from successes. Everyone who plays sports knows that. I stress good writing skills, so grades suffer from poor examples in my classes. Students learn from rewriting and the experiences make them better writers. You probably remember the writing "rules" that you learned the best because of mistakes you made in class.

Another example of learning from mistakes is a well-known pizza chain. Some years ago, Domino's Pizza had an incident with a customer who complained that they did not make their pizza right. They asked him to show them. He did. It took awhile, but both Domino's and this customer learned a lot. Domino's then gave the customer free pizza for life because they felt that he had been able to improve their processes. Domino's used their mistake to improve their long-term customer relations. If you look back at your college years, I know that you will remember the mistakes that caused the most lasting and positive impression on you, mistakes that made you a better person.

An excellent recent example of a leader who used integrity to push a difficult admission is Timothy Flynn. He was advised just days before he took the top job at KPMG LLP, a major accounting and consulting firm, that the firm faced imminent criminal indictment over tax shelters it used to sell. For years, KPMG had denied impropriety and used its substantial legal defenses to do so. But Flynn wanted to take a different road. Just before meeting with the Justice Department, Flynn told his advisors *"You only get one chance to make a first impression at a meeting like this."*[20] He said, *"I think we just admit wrongdoing and accept responsibility."* In return, the Justice Department let KPMG know that they were willing to discuss a settlement. In the end, it cost the firm $456 million and several partners left, but KPMG survived. It was clearly the right thing to do to admit wrongdoing and face the consequences. Indeed, the consequences of admitting wrongdoing were far less than they would have been had the firm collapsed. Flynn certainly used integrity, persistence, and discipline to see the firm through this crisis.

Johnson & Johnson recently discovered wrongdoing in one of its subsidiary companies, which was improperly marketing a psychotic drug for use in children. Because J&J caught the problem and reported it before the government did, they will likely not be charged and escape fines[21]. You can imagine how much this would have cost if they have tried to hide the activity.

At some point in your life, you will probably (I say probably, but not necessarily) get a ticket for some traffic infraction. I remember "earning" a speeding ticket for going fifty miles per hour in a twenty-five-mile zone on a wide street, with no traffic, at three in the afternoon. It did not matter that the next street over had a speed limit of forty, or that I was not endangering anyone in that one-half mile part of the street. I was guilty. But, I still whined. It wasn't fair. The cop should have been going after "real" speeders. You know what? I broke the law. It is that simple. I learned that not accepting responsibility for my own actions was pretty stupid.

My students have found that I am more understanding when they come to me with the "mea culpa" of what they did than when they try to create a story of why they could not accomplish their assignment. After all, we were all college students at one time, and we do remember that stuff happens. Just tell the truth. Your future bosses will also be more understanding and appreciative of your integrity.

One of the books that I frequently use in my marketing classes is the classic best seller, *How to Win Friends and Influence People*, by Dale Carnegie[22], written in 1936. Taking the Dale Carnegie public relations course was one of the smartest investments I ever made, even though it cost me eight hundred dollars (in 1983 dollars)! Carnegie talked a lot about admitting mistakes in his book. *"Any fool can try to defend his or her mistakes—and most fools do—but it raises one above the herd and gives one a feeling of nobility and exultation to admit one's mistakes"* (p.139). Carnegie also said, "*If we know we are going to be rebuked anyhow, isn't it far better to beat the other person to it and do it ourselves?"* (p.137) I know I make a lot of mistakes in class, from the syllabus to mistaking one student for another. I hope that I properly apologize for those mistakes before students have to call me on them.

We have enough lying in this world. The coverage of it exhausts the media. You can look back at the lying that cost Richard Nixon the presidency, the cover-up that forced CBS anchorman Dan Rather to retire, and many others. Telling the truth would have been far less damaging in the long run. I hope that these examples will convince you that accepting responsibility truly is the right thing to do.

Integrity, Persistence and Discipline

5

Take Responsibility, sometimes when it isn't Your Fault

The buck stops at the top, even when it isn't the fault of the person at the top. This is a very important part of the responsibility you bear as educated people.

A number of years ago, a truck driver who worked for the company where I was National Sales Manager got into a physical altercation with one of the store managers at our biggest account (this means he slugged him). I drove down to San Diego and apologized to the store manager. I have no doubt that the store manager deserved what the truck driver gave him, but my actions had a good outcome as that store manager eventually became the category buyer for the customer and I called on him. I never had any problems with him. But, even if that had not been the outcome, the responsibility for that behavior stopped with me. Managers must take responsibility for actions all the way down the line.

One of the most famous examples of fallout reaching the top is the 1991 Tailhook scandal at the Naval Academy in Annapolis, Maryland[23]. In total, one hundred nineteen Navy and twenty-one Marine Corps officers were cited for incidents relating to sexual assault. Though none ever went to trial, both the Secretary of the Navy and the Chief Naval Officer either resigned or retired. Ultimately, the careers of fourteen admirals and almost three hundred aviators were scuttled or damaged by Tailhook. The integrity to take responsibility for something that happens on your watch is deeply ingrained into the United States Military. Although the military is well known for discipline, even discipline is useless without integrity in leadership.

"Owning the customer's problem" is something that I often discuss when I lead customer service seminars. We know that a greater percentage of customers will do business again if a problem is solved than would be loyal if there were no problem at all[24]. Calling a customer back to tell him or her that you don't have the answer yet is almost as important as having the answer. It is good for the company, it is good for the customer, and it adds to important team relationships. Customers often care more about the effort you make for them than the actual outcome (remember, knowing how much you care before caring how much you know).

At the university, our financial aid staff has gone through a program to accomplish a seamless route for the customer (student). By looking at the whole student experience, they have created a large improvement in student attitudes toward their services. The staff has learned not to just transfer a student, but to make sure that the problem is on the way to being fixed. The benefit of this behavior is and will be a happier student and more committed alumni.

Ritz Carlton is probably the gold standard when it comes to customer service personnel. They know that they are "ladies and gentlemen" serving "ladies and gentlemen." They take responsibility for problems on the spot and front desk personnel have a certain amount they can spend to correct the problem. As customers remember their last experience, Ritz Carlton works hard to make sure that each one is a good one.

Once you take responsibility for something that did not go right, it will take less time to get to the bottom of the problem and fix it. Once people stop blaming each other for a problem, they can move on to put into place processes designed to prevent a recurrence. Moving toward a solution is always more likely to produce a positive result than spending energy finding someone else to blame, even if someone else is to blame.

Integrity, Persistence and Discipline

6

Embrace Change and Look for Opportunities

You have heard that there are two things you can count on—death and taxes. Add change to that because you can count on it, more now than ever. Just as products you have grown up with (computers, cell phones) have displaced products from an earlier era (typewriters, land phone lines), more than 50 percent of the jobs you will hold have not even been invented yet.

Your skills must be portable and you must keep educating yourself. The end of your college education was really only the beginning. When Home Depot became a major factor in home center retailing and refused to buy through distribution (intermediaries), the distributors fought that change by threatening their suppliers. Guess who won? The market (read: customers) will decide where the best values are and that will determine the future.

Be aware of your surroundings, of what new skills you can gain, of new market opportunities. I recently had a former student come in to ask me to give him advice on opening his own real estate office. He has exactly one and one-half year's experience. I asked him if he reads the *Wall Street Journal.* "No," he answered. I told him that was a good way to keep up on what is happening in his industry.

Keep reading and expect that your world will continue to offer new opportunities. But you have to "prime the pump," meaning you have to give it some water before it will start a continuous flow. The best way to discover opportunities is if you are ready for them, watching for them. The Federal Express story is well known to many people, that Fred Smith wrote a paper at Yale on his idea for an express mail service. The professor did not think much of the idea and gave him a "C." The rest is history. He saw an opportunity and developed it. Recently, FedEx bought Kinkos so that they could offer all their services at Kinkos' stores and compete with UPS stores. They did that because they saw the signals of home businesses and the need to bundle services such as shipping and printing. By reading and paying attention to how change can give you opportunities, you will encounter more opportunities. Be ready for them and embrace them. To do otherwise dooms you.

One of the best stories of opportunity grabbing is that of Howard Schultz, who was a salesman for a kitchenware company when he visited a small coffee shop in Seattle's Pike Place Market that just happened to be buying a lot of his product[25]. He noticed an opportunity to capitalize on what he saw as a special kind of place. Today, Starbucks has over 7,000 stores and is growing internationally. Schultz created his own opportunity, took a lot of risks, and has made a lot of people rich. He did it because he was passionate about his idea and people followed him for that reason. Recently, Starbucks has added computer terminals to many of their stores, another response to change. We also have Howard Schultz to thank for basically inventing the gourmet coffee industry in this country. Today, more than 70 percent of coffee purchased is gourmet coffee and the makers of Maxwell House (Kraft) and Folgers (Procter & Gamble) are struggling to catch up because they missed the signals of change.

Don't be afraid to try things you have never tried before. That is the way you learn. Although I don't advocate telling an employer you have experience with something you don't, the willingness to try it may be important. For instance, if someone asks you to prepare an executive briefing and you have never done it before, accept the assignment and then research it so that you can do it. You will find that employers expect college graduates to be able to do a lot of things you may not remember from specific classes. But you did study them and you can do them. College teaches you to learn and to know where there is information. The message we get from employers is that they are looking for the willingness to find and learn skills that may not be automatically apparent when a need arises.

The previous example about the Hilton valet who took it upon himself to find out how to fix a customer problem is why that young man will be promoted over and over again.

Michael Dell did exactly what Howard Shultz did; he tried a new business model created around direct customer sales of computers. But, Dell *"acquired too much middle-aged fat and lost the intense focus and drive that made it an icon."*[26] Dell also did not notice as customers increasingly wanted to go into a store to look at the product rather than just view options online; they also moved away from desktop computers to laptops, which Dell does not promote. No business model lasts forever, and the creators must always be seeking the evolutionary potential of what is new now but will not be new forever. Some of the companies that sparked major market changes in the 1990's but have had to adapt in this century include Wal-Mart, which is struggling with a mature business model in many markets; Southwest Airlines, which is facing nimble rivals as they adopt even newer ways to transport customers profitably; and Enron, which touted a trading strategy that collapsed in tragedy[27].

I want you to think that you can change the world because you have to believe it to do it! Think about Walt Disney. With his cartoons, he did change the world, created millions of jobs and made a lot of people rich, not to mention happy at "The Happiest Place on Earth." Or Chester Carlson, who saw the possibility of commercially copying documents long before even the mighty IBM thought it possible. Both of these men had imagination. They had persistence; they had discipline. From what I know about them, they also had great integrity. You can have integrity and lag on discipline, but you can't successfully have the other two and come in second in integrity.

In Zig Ziglar's latest book, *Better than Good*, he quotes Joe Sabah in reminding us that *"You don't have to be great to start. But you have to start to be great."*[28] This is why the willingness to chance failure and to welcome opportunity is truly the secret to those who reach the highest of objectives.

> ***"An optimist sees an opportunity in every calamity; a pessimist sees a calamity in every opportunity."***
>
> **—Winston Churchill**

Employers will respect your willingness to take on responsibility. It is called initiative and sets you apart from people who expect to be told how to do everything. When I am asked to write a letter of recommendation for a former student, "initiative" is always one of the traits they ask about. They want to know—"Am I going to have to watch this person all the time? Am I going to have to guide him or her every step of the way?" Employers prize people who are creative and take initiative in accomplishing tasks. You need to take control of your own destiny, not expect others to do it.

One of the best examples of persistence and discipline comes from the following purported 2001 *Houston Chronicle* story about famous violinist Itzhak Perlman's experience giving a concert at Lincoln Center:

> *"If you have ever been to a Perlman concert, you know that getting on stage is no small achievement for him. He was stricken with polio as a child, and so he has braces on both legs and walks with the aid of two crutches. To see him walk across the stage one step at a time, painfully and slowly, is an awesome sight.*
>
> *He walks painfully, yet majestically, until he reaches his chair. Then he sits down, slowly puts his crutches on the floor, undoes the clasps on his legs, tucks one foot back and extends the other foot forward. Then he bends down and picks up the violin, puts it under his chin and proceeds to play.*
>
> *By now, the audience is used to this ritual. They sit quietly while he makes his way across the stage to his chair. They remain reverently silent while he undoes the clasps on his legs. They wait until he is ready to play.*
>
> *But this time, something went wrong. Just as he finished the first few bars, one of the strings on his violin broke. You could hear it snap-it went off like gunfire across the room. There was no mistaking what that sound meant. There was no mistaking what he had to do. We figured that he*

would have to get up, put on the clasps again, pick up his crutches and limp his way off stage—to either find another violin or else find another string for this one. But he didn't. Instead, he waited a moment, closed his eyes and then signaled the conductor to begin again.

The orchestra began, and he played from where he left off. And he played with such passion and such power and such purity, as they had never heard before.

Of course, anyone knows that it is impossible to play a symphonic work with just three strings. I know that and you know that, but that night Itzhak Perlman refused to know that.

You could see him modulating, changing, and re-composing the piece in his head. At one point, it sounded like he was de-tuning the strings to get new sounds from them that they had never made before. When he finished, there was an awesome silence in the room. And then people rose and cheered. There was an extraordinary outburst of applause from every corner of the auditorium. We were all on our feet, screaming and cheering; doing everything we could to show how much we appreciated what he had done.

He smiled, wiped the sweat from his brow, raised his bow to quiet Us, and then he said-not boastfully, but in a quiet, pensive reverent tone—"You know, sometimes it is the artist's task to find out how much music you can make with what you have left."

What a powerful line that is. It has stayed in my mind ever since I heard it. And who knows? Perhaps that is the definition of life-not just for artists but for all of us. Here is a man who has prepared all his life to make music on a violin of four strings, who, all of a sudden, in the middle of a concert, finds himself with only three strings; so he makes music with three strings, and the music he made that night with just three strings was more beautiful, more sacred, more memorable, than any that he had ever made before, when he had four strings.

So, perhaps our task in this shaky, bewildering world in which we live is to make music, at first with all that we have, and then, when that is no longer possible, to make music with what we have left.[29]

Now, by way of total disclosure, there are a number of sources that question whether this event happened, primarily because of a lack of newspaper coverage in New York, where the concert was held. I have chosen to leave in the reference because Mr. Perlman has used persistence and discipline in his craft, even while facing the challenges of a disabling physical condition. Even if this story is not true of this particular instance, Itzak Perlman exemplifies the message in this book.

The future will be built on innovation and technology. Few areas of the country more embody those concepts than Silicon Valley, once known as the Santa Clara Valley. But how did it get that way? In 1956, without knowing what was on the horizon, Robert Noyce, the future inventor of the silicon integrated circuit, left a job at Bell Labs to travel to the future Silicon Valley to take a job with a start-up founded by William Shockley, who won the Nobel Prize for the invention of the transistor. The job turned out to be in a converted apricot barn. This was a gutsy move, especially for someone with a wife and two children. But Intel has captivated and created business after business and opportunity after opportunity for thousands of people. It would not have happened had the founders not seen opportunity and been willing to risk their finances to create something[30].

Recently, in my senior business seminar, the students were giving presentations about their strategic simulation game. I talk frequently about consistency and sticking with your plan. One of my students boldly asked me if it was always (yikes!) a good idea to stick with a strategy. Well, I said, it all depends on the environment. For instance, Kodak stuck with their film strategy and almost lost their business with the introduction of digital cameras. But going back to 1839, when Charles Goodyear accidentally discovered vulcanization, he doggedly pushed through financial hardships because he believed that this discovery would benefit other people. He said, *"I am not disposed to complain that I have planted and others have gathered the fruits. A man has cause for regret only when he sows and no one reaps."*[31] You have to keep believing in what you are trying to do, because there will be many failures on the way to success. Success requires a hearty soul. Being prepared to capitalize on change is the most important trait in that success.

Integrity, Persistence and Discipline

7

You can't have it all, but You can Live a Glorious and Fulfilled Life

I used to talk about Martha Stewart and how much I disliked her "you can have it all after you shoot and stuff the family dinner" attitude. My students always teased me because they thought I was unfair. I probably was (mea culpa). But, in reality, you are probably not going to be able to create a five-course meal for hundreds unless you have a lot of help (which she does). Within reason, however, your opportunities are also endless.

You will have to decide how to pace yourself. Our generation (the baby boomers) tried to have it all, the big house, the boat, the kids, and the exciting careers. The price? Daycare. The "latch-key" generation. Heavy debt. I am seeing young people realize that they have to make their choices more wisely than we did. They are spending time with their children and attending their soccer games, even if it means saying no to a lucrative job transfer. You have the opportunity to avoid the mistakes my generation made, to weigh the value of your family.

You are smart enough to make good choices for your family and for yourself. You can decide what "having it all" means. I have always told my students that if you have people who love you and you know where your next meal is coming from, you really do have it all. Given that one billion people in the world live in poverty, those two things really are a lot.

Don't compare yourself with others. We are all more skillful at some tasks than others. In a recent speech, I talked about Zoe Koplowitz, the last runner in the New York marathon yearly, meaning she comes in after twenty-nine thousand other people and it takes her more than twenty-nine hours to finish the race. Because Koplowitz suffers from multiple sclerosis and uses Canadian crutches, it takes her a loooong time. As a former runner and also a multiple sclerosis patient, is that a goal I should set for myself? Do I compare myself to Zoe Koplowitz? No. I don't need that kind of accomplishment to validate my goals. Yes, envy invades the internal yearnings of all of us at times; it "is part of the secret life."[32] It is harmless unless it leads to harm to another person or society. I predict that, as you get older, you will no longer envy certain people who have a lot of money or a good looking spouse—you will start to appreciate what you do have and refuse to sacrifice it for riches or beauty. You need to pick what goals you want to accomplish in life (home, family, happiness) and go for them. Work on what is important to you, not to other people. Money cannot buy happiness, but relationships can.

You can live a glorious life because you can choose what is important to you. Your choices will change as you mature. When I was in my twenties, I loved to cook and sew. I made Raggedy Ann dolls for my friends when they had children and I made suits for my first husband. I also cooked all day long for guests. That was part of my life then. It isn't now. Now I choose other avocations to take up my free time, such as writing and volunteering. You will go through the same transition, but make sure it is one that you choose. Don't do things because a friend does them or because your parents tell you that you should. There are many opportunities that will make you happy. Don't make the mistake of thinking your friends or siblings have "everything." You get to choose what "everything" means.

You get to choose what "everything" means because you live in a country where immigrants are four times more likely to become millionaires than native-born Americans. You live in a country where *"Every law-abiding citizen enjoys freedom of thought and freedom of deed unequaled anywhere in the world."*[33] You can get the education you need, regardless of your background or your income. Opportunities are endless and, if you aren't successful somewhere or in some profession, nothing is stopping you from moving and changing professions! But you have to be prepared, constantly aware of opportunities and what they require of you. Franklin Roosevelt served three terms as President of the United States, though he was crippled by polio in 1921. Helen Keller graduated Cum Laude from Radcliff

College, though not able to hear or see. According to well-known speaker Roger Dawson, "The secret of power performers is they take charge of their lives."[34]

In school, you learned that the top 5 percent of families in terms of income got more than 21 percent of the total. Does that sound fair? Well, you also get to choose where you will be in that earning curve. The ability to be at the top or the bottom is purely a matter of education, persistence, and performance. It is your choice whether the discrepancy is fair or not.

Of course, life is not always going to turn out the way you want or expect it to. Sometimes you really do have to make lemonade out of a lemon, but that will get you closer still to where you want to be! The saying "when one door closes, another one opens" really is true. For many years, I wanted to work for the Masco Corporation, the preeminent manufacturer in the hardware/home center industry. If I had not been fired from one job because of a re-organization, the opportunity would not have come up to talk to them, and indeed spend the last nine years of my corporate career there.

"Things turn out best for the people who make the best of the way things turn out."

—John Wooden

I was a Board Member for the Southern California Chapter of the National Multiple Sclerosis Society at the time that the Marilyn Hilton MS Achievement Center was established at UCLA to assist patients with wellness and exercise. The family of the founder of the Hilton hotel chain has been an incredible donor to many philanthropic causes. Mrs. Hilton, who passed way in 2004 from multiple sclerosis, had this philosophy:

> *"You don't look back at what might have been. You just accept the condition that life has presented and you make the best of what you have."*[35]

Of course, that is the same thing as making lemonade out of lemons, something I must warn you that you will face plenty of in your career. But treat each one as a challenge and you will be surprised at how much less sour they are!

Success for you will be what you choose. You may think that "success" means a lot of money or an impressive job title. Success is what makes *you* happy and fulfilled, no more and no less. You can escape the false trappings of what some people think is success. If you escape that, you will be far more successful than if you chase a label that does not fit you. At this point, you are probably vulnerable to some of those "get rich quick" schemes, but I plead with you to take the long-term approach. Your education took about four years, and now you appreciate why it took so long (or, at least, you will soon). Don't worry about making those dreams come true right away. I had a student whose goal was to become a millionaire by the time he was twenty-five. That is a pretty empty dream and one that does not mean he will be truly successful and happy. His relationships will make him happy and his satisfaction with his work and the contribution he makes to the mission of his work will make him successful. Not magic, but the key to success all the same.

Unfortunately, the media fills our world with images of rich and famous personalities. Are we supposed to idolize someone who memorizes lines from a script and happens to be good at delivering them? The real heroes, the ones we should be fashioning our actions after, are guarding and teaching our children. They are risking their lives in a far off land to make sure that freedom comes to people who have been denied it for centuries. They are everyday heroes and they are all around you. I am very concerned (and I voice this to my students all the time) that the movies make you think that everyone needs to be slim, with perfect teeth. I've known lots of slim people with perfect teeth who were terribly unhappy. So, if you think that you should set your sights on a career or role model that does not reach your heart, talk to someone who has common sense and maturity. They have been there and they know that what glitters is very seldom pure gold.

Find something you are passionate about. You may not find it right now. In fact, it took me until age twenty-six to find, after a couple of jobs in the banking industry, that what I really wanted to do was sales training.

I tried to get jobs in training after we moved to the west coast, but banking in California in those days was not very sophisticated when it came to sales training. So I pursued training in the other jobs I took and eventually found that teaching sales was one of the most gratifying things I could do. Don't be impatient about finding the "right" thing. Just explore and try different things. Exploring and responding to opportunities will allow you to live a wonderfully fulfilling life even if you can't "have it all" in the traditional sense.

My ninety-one-year-old father lives in a very nice retirement community in Springfield, Virginia. He has many friends whose careers were rewarding and productive. He recently sent me the advice one of the residents there gave him. It is as good a guide to the "good life" as I can imagine:

1. *To follow the ethical principle in all matters.*
2. *To continue intellectual and moral growth.*
3. *To be productive in my work, striving constantly for professional competence.*
4. *To be confident yet humble; strong yet compassionate; decisive, yet sympathetic.*
5. *To be ready to assist those persons deserving or requesting help.*
6. *To be concerned with the affairs of men rather than things.*
7. *To be a good husband and father and provide a secure home*
8. *To appreciate beauty in the arts and the joy of creativity.*
9. *To follow the mood of loving best suited to the preservation of health.*
10. *To live fully, striving constantly to use time productively.(Anonymous)*

Integrity, Persistence and Discipline

8

Cherish Your Relationships

When George Herbert Walker Bush was President of the United States (1988 to 1992), his wife, Barbara, was invited to give the commencement address at Wellesley College. There was a public outcry that she did not have her own credentials, but I think she said something as important as anyone could have to those graduates: "Your relationships will be important in ten years; your current grades will not." Every piece of research I have done on employer needs has confirmed this fact. Keep in touch with your classmates. Don't hold grudges. As you mature, your circle of friends will change. Happiness is improved when people have a lot of friends—health is improved as well!

I spent a lot of time some years ago studying Executive Management MBA programs. In this world of on-line education, it sticks out that the most important benefit to the over two hundred people I studied was their teams. They cherished and continued to socialize with their teams long after they graduated. Out of many of these relationships came very lucrative business opportunities.

You will find that the atmosphere in your workplace, the culture, will quickly rise to the top as important benefits in a possible job opportunity. When I ask students what they want in a job, money invariably tops the list. But, when we explore the priorities they really have, they realize that how they feel about their jobs and their accomplishments within those organizations will truly be the most important aspect to them. Positive relationships with co-workers contribute to productivity and happiness on the job. They also contribute to longer life.

I have already mentioned the "Credo" of Johnson & Johnson. The reason it fits in here is that the culture of Johnson & Johnson is very much built around their Credo and they hire people who will safeguard it. My relationships with the other twelve members of my sales team at J&J were very special and I still, twenty-nine years later, keep in touch with some of them. Choosing a company that fits your own values will enhance those relationships.

Make sure that you are nice to people on the way up because you might need them on the way down! As your career grows, you will meet numerous people whose jobs will change, as will yours. Some will become your superiors, some your employees, and some will stay professional colleagues. If you treat everyone, the janitor, the mailroom person, the grocery checker, as you would want to be treated, you will be blessed with a lot of friends in a lot of places. I remember when I was a Regional Manager for Peerless Faucet and we had a meeting in Indianapolis, from which I was flying to another city. The driver that Peerless used also worked in the mailroom and I saw him whenever I visited the corporate headquarters. Because he was driving me to the airport from the meeting, I asked the director of marketing if he could have lunch with us. No, she said, that would not be appropriate. I have never forgotten that because he was basically doing the same job I was—working to sell faucets. His job certainly did not pay as well as mine, but he was there to support the efforts of the entire corporation. If you remember this story, you will make many friends as you pursue your career. In my opinion, he was not a driver; he was a partner.

An even better story that illustrates the above point is "who packed your parachute?"

> *"Charles Plumb was a U.S. Navy jet pilot in Vietnam. After 75 combat missions, his plane was destroyed by a surface-to-air missile. Plumb ejected and parachuted into enemy hands. He was captured and spent 6 years in a communist Vietnamese prison. He survived the ordeal and now lectures on lessons learned from that experience.*
>
> *One day, when Plumb and his wife were sitting in a restaurant, a man at another table came up and said, "You're Plumb! You flew jet fighters in Vietnam from the aircraft carrier Kitty Hawk. You were shot down!"*

> *"How in the world did you know that?" asked Plumb. "I packed your parachute," the man replied. Plumb gasped in surprise and gratitude. The man pumped his hand and said, "I guess it worked!" Plumb assured him, "It sure did. If your chute hadn't worked, I wouldn't be here today."*[36]

The point of this is that many people are involved in making sure that we are safe and comfortable on a daily basis—people who work on street lights, people who clean our offices, people who prepare our meals. It takes a lot of dedicated people to put an airman into an airplane and it takes a lot of dedicated people to provide meals for people in hospitals. Do we take the time to recognize and appreciate our relationships with these behind the scenes workers?

Integrity, Persistence and Discipline

9

Network

The vast majority of the fourteen jobs I have held in my career, spanning thirty-six years, have been obtained through networking. Once I had lost a job and received a call from a competitive sales organization, giving me a tip that resulted in a job offer. That covers two of my points: relationships and networking! Join organizations, go to church, volunteer. A recent article in the *Wall Street Journal* stated *"If you want to stand out, join the crowd."* The article gives several examples of people who got interviews and jobs because they were members of a club or association.[37] Many associations also post job opportunities on their web sites, as I do for the members of our chapter of the American Marketing Association. If you want to meet someone in this country, it takes only three people to reach him or her. If you want to go to work for Disney, I know someone who knows someone who can make that contact. If you want to start your own business, I have lots of contacts there! The newspaper is not the best way to find a job, networking is.

When I was working on my MBA in the 1980s, I heard a tape by a woman who had an interesting story to tell. She was working for Hagger Slacks in Dallas, in 1968. Haggar actually coined the term "slacks." For the ladies in my readership, Hagger Slacks in 1968 was not a place that promised ready advancement to women. Well, this woman wanted to go into advertising and she knew she would not get that chance at Hagger. So, she quit her job, moved to New York, and set about finding opportunities in the advertising field. She combined passion with persistence when she invited the presidents of the top 20 advertising agencies in New York to breakfast! Every one of them called her. She did not have breakfast with any of them, but ended up getting a referral to American Express, where her career soared. This story may seem like a fairy tale, but it happens like that all the time!

I worked for the Masco Corporation for almost ten years in four different divisions. During one taxi ride in Chicago, where major trade shows are held, the woman I had agreed to share the cab with told me she had a colleague who very much wanted to work for Masco. He was from Michigan, where Masco is based, had an MBA from an Ivy League school, and needed an introduction. I did not know this woman and I did not know her friend, but her position in the industry gave her some credibility. I did send his resume to Masco. He was eventually hired and it turned out to be one of the best hiring decisions that Masco made. This all came from networking.

More recently, I was searching for a prospective account for Pomona Valley Workshop, a local employer of developmentally disabled adults where I serve on the Board of Directors. I was very frustrated because Pomona Valley Workshop (PVW) had lost their long-term customer, Stone Container, for which they sorted pizza boxes for Domino's Pizza. Stone Container automated their processes, which left PVW with a $10,000 monthly loss. With state support decreasing and many employers going offshore with assembly jobs, there seemed few prospects to save PVW. Then I remembered Joel Rosen, who worked for me at Leviton manufacturing more than 20 years ago. Joel is 71 years old now, in semi-retirement, and working for a company called L.H. Dottie, which imports and sells hardware such as nuts and bots for retail and wholesale accounts. It turned out that L.H.Dottie hires many employers of developmentally disabled adults for their production lines. One phone call led to a visit by PVW to L.H. Dottie and the first truckload pick-up in two days! PVW has a system to enable the developmentally disabled workers to actually produce products, making a contribution to the workforce and feeling good about themselves. It is a win-win situation for all concerned and it all came about because of networking! LH Dottie has told PVW that they are their best vendor! At the recent annual meeting of PVW, everyone was excited about the events that came together to allow us to serve this very deserving population. And it was networking, plus a whole lot of persistence, that provided the path. I believe strongly in the integrity of the people who manage PVW and the discipline and persistence they use to meet the goals of their consumers every day.

The Tipping Point, How Little Things Can Make a Big Difference[38] created quite a stir when it remained a national bestseller for many weeks. In his chapter on "*The Law of the Few*", Malcolm Gladwell discusses the well-known ride of Paul Revere in1775 to warn of the impending march by the British on the town of Lexington, Massachusetts. Gladwell says, *"Paul Revere's ride is perhaps the most famous historical example of a word-of-mouth epidemic."* But what our children don't study in American History is that William Dawes, a fellow revolutionary, also set out to warn the citizenry. The difference, and the "tipping point" was that Revere was "connected"; he knew lots of people. In Dawes' case, he was not "connected" with enough local militia leaders to cause a "tipping point" of massive reaction, as in the case of Paul Revere's ride. Just this example, and the important outcome of this particular example of networking, should convince you that good networking could have an incredible effect on your career.

You need to manage and cultivate your networks like a fine friend. Make sure you are positively contributing to the network. According to the *Wall Street Journal*, *"If you aren't giving back more than you're getting from networking, then you're a baby in the job-search process."*[39] And, in the glorious game of life, what you give is what you will get back.

You need to add follow-up and persistence to networking as well. If that young man had not continued to contact me about his resume, nothing would have happened with regard to his desire to work for Masco. He needed the luck of networking and the persistence of follow-up to make his dream come true. That is where trade associations, community service groups and church memberships come in handy. Harvard is well known for the contacts that its students can use in their careers. You can make your own contacts, but you have to be strategic about it and look for opportunities.

Integrity, Persistence and Discipline

10

Remember that You are Self-employed

No matter who signs your check, you are self-employed. In other words, if you don't show up for work, how long will they keep paying you? Do you get the picture? Many of our graduates think they have a year or more to prove their mettle in the workplace, but that is not true. We are all self-employed from day one.

You are self-employed because you are responsible for what you earn and how long you earn it. Your employer, even if it is you, is really only interested in what you are going to do tomorrow. Don't fall into the trap of making a great sale and expecting to profit from it indefinitely. As a matter of fact, the largest sale I ever made, $450,000, came on the same day I was fired in a re-organization. Also remember that the environment is always changing. Your self-employed self must be aware of changes that require changes in your skills and education.

Now that you have accepted your true employment status, remember that you have ten seconds to make an impression. Your dress, your appearance, and your communication skills all contribute to that impression. If you watch people on the street greet each other, you can tell the difference between the "what's up" and the "good morning." It is one of respect. Everywhere you go exist opportunities to put forward the successful you, the successful self-employed you.

My students think I am "different." Perhaps that is because I have been where they are going for more than half my life. Sometimes I worry that I am too strict about their need to be responsible, but I felt validated when I received this letter from a student who entered military service upon graduation:

Dear Dr. Dietz,

I just wanted to take this opportunity to say thank you. Thank you for being you. You are truly one of the best instructors I have ever had. I have learned so much in both your courses. I may not have been the best student, always on time, got the best grades, etc. But I can tell you that you have prepared me to go out into that nasty "real world" and succeed. Thank you for being that strict, stubborn, yet compassionate and caring professor. I could always count on you to hold me accountable and let me know when I was wrong and also support me, understand and respect my military obligations. You have made an impact on my college/learning experience in a very positive way and I am forever thankful for that. Yea, you might say, "Hey, Matt, I'm just doing my job." But, compared to other instructors I've had, I think you go above and beyond doing your job. Thank you once again for being you. I am honored to have been your student. See you at graduation.

Sincerely, Matt Jackson

Although it took a few knocks on the head (not literally) for Matt to realize that I was doing him a favor by preparing him to go beyond the classroom, he is excelling in his military career and welcoming the challenges it contains. He knows he is self-employed. I am very proud of him.

Do you want to be great? Winston Churchill said *"responsibility is the price of greatness."* In other words, if you want all that this degree can provide for you, you must take the responsibility to go out and get it. Other people do not control your future. You do. Now is the time to understand and accept the fact that circumstances will combine to challenge you. There is no doubt about that. But if you approach your career with the knowledge that your success is dependent on your own effort, you can avoid the "victim mentality" that paralyzes many in the workforce today.

Integrity, Persistence and Discipline

11

Protect Your Brand

This may seem like a strange addition, but you are a brand and protecting it is the most important thing you can and must do every day. Remember that your brand value lies in the perception of other people. Whether right or wrong in terms of their viewpoint of you, your brand defines you.

Integrity, persistence and discipline all fit into your brand as people know you in direct proportion to the measure of these ingredients. As a salesman, nothing is more important to me than my integrity. No order, no job, no amount of money. Don't compromise what makes you saleable and different. In the book *The Innovator's Solution*[40], the authors discuss the "jobs" that people hire companies, people, and products to perform. They talk about milkshakes. What are the jobs that people "hire" milkshakes to perform? It is interesting to note the frequency with which people "hire" milkshakes because of their portability and the ability to consume them with the one hand a driver usually has free. Along that line, what people are hiring you to do, what makes you saleable, is your suitability to perform the task they need done. But your brand has to be right—it has to have the right appearance (no nose rings, please), the right attitude and ability to communicate, the right educational qualifications, and the right skills.

If you think of it this way, I hope you realize that protecting your brand is a life-long endeavor. Once that brand is tarnished, through poor performance or reputation, it takes a long time to polish it back to its original luster, if ever. Integrity, persistence, and discipline are integral parts of a sustainable brand. You have to polish your brand much more frequently than your family silver!

A brand identifies the maker of a product or service. It serves to reduce risk, help consumers identify products that they trust, and signal consistency in performance, service, or whatever the brand is positioned to communicate. Coca Cola is the most valuable brand in the world, followed by such venerable names as McDonald's, Microsoft, and General Electric. However, even Coca Cola has had its missteps in this area. Former CEO Douglas Ivester lost his job in part due to incidents like failing to respond to an occurrence in Belgium where some glue on pallets used to transport Coke products sickened some school children. Ivester, unlike Jim Burke at Johnson & Johnson (remember the Tylenol tragedy?), failed to fly to Belgium and address the situation, whether it involved Coca Cola's wrongdoing or not. As stated before, the brand is the perception of the people who purchase it (or hire it). Arrogant disregard for this fact has cost more than one manager his or her job.

Your brand, what makes you different, is what employers will buy. They will associate anything they hear about you from references as part of the brand you are offering them. Every association with your brand is important. If people are watching when you don't think they are and you behave poorly, the impact on your brand and your future can be deadly. You are always representing yourself, always.

Remember this when you are representing your employer at a convention, off-site meeting or on the phone. As you have only ten seconds to make a first impression, the value of your brand can be lost just as easily if you do or say something that damages the brand your employer bought. Your reputation will follow you throughout your career. Although formal references will only detail your hire date and salary, most good managers will not hire someone unless they can get a good reference from someone they trust. This means a good, "off-the record" reference. Remember that the tone of voice a reference gives can be very enlightening.

> ***"A brand is a living entity and it is enriched or undermined cumulatively over time, the product of a thousand small gestures."***
>
> ***—Michael Eisner, former CEO, Disney***

Your brand communicates whether you are trustworthy and act with integrity and respect for your employer and those with whom you do business. People with strong brands don't burn bridges with their employers. As I worked for four different divisions of the Masco corporation over nine years, I know that my "brand" is what enabled me to be considered for positions that came available across Masco's businesses.

Think of names such as Donald Trump, Paris Hilton, Colin Powell. However you feel about these people, there is an emotional response that identifies how you feel about them and the ideas they are selling. It will be exactly the same for you as you move through your career. When people hear your name, do they think "trustworthy," "likeable," and "dependable?" As we know that a brand such as Tiffany can affect what people are willing to pay for a product, do you see how this can affect your future income stream?

In a crowded job market, what distinguishes you from other people may make the difference in a hiring decision. Believe it or not, I once competed with nineteen men for a national sales job and was hired, according to the Vice President, because I wrote a thank you note. That apparently set me aside as being different and more serious than any of the other candidates. In the same vein, one of our award-winning students lost out on a job with one of the country's largest accounting firms because she did not write a follow-up note. Recently, another student went on an interview wearing Capri pants. She could not understand why that was not appropriate. Sometimes it is that simple. When the title of this book mentioned the "3 simple secrets", that is what I meant!

It takes many good deeds to build a good reputation, and only one bad one to lose it.

—Benjamin Franklin

Make sure your brand is true and consistent. If you are known for your enthusiasm, remember that you are always on stage. If you are known for your analytical skills, keep them current. Your "brand" will precede you and follow you.

The following anonymous poem, read by former Girl Scouts of America CEO Frances Hasselbein at our 2007 graduation ceremonies, ends this chapter with the punch I intend:

Be careful of your thoughts, for your thoughts become your words.
Be careful of your deeds, for your deeds become your habits.
Be careful of your habits, for your habits become your character.
Be careful of your character, for your character becomes your destiny.

Integrity, Persistence, and Discipline

12

You will always Learn Something, Sometimes in the Unlikeliest of Places

When I graduated from college in 1971, I was among many in the first wave of baby boomer generation to do so; consequently, there was a lot of competition. After a lengthy search, I obtained a job as a secretary for Girl Scouts of Rhode Island. (My Dad always told me to learn to type!) After graduating Cum Laude from the University of Rhode Island in three years, I was very disappointed in the fact that I could not land a job that would use my college education, or so I thought. Does that sound familiar? Instead, I spent much time separating ZIP codes and typing letters for the executive director, who had a penchant for run-on sentences. One day, seeing my frustration at this job, my supervisor gave me one of the most important pieces of advice I have ever gotten: "You will always learn something." That statement came back to me when I read a recent interview with Sandra Day O'Connor, who retired in 2005 after serving as the first female Supreme Court Justice. She mentioned how much things have changed for female lawyers since she graduated from Stanford in 1952. During her first interview, the interviewer asked O'Connor how well she typed! If she could type well, he might be able to get her a job as a legal secretary.[41] Apparently she did not take that job, but we all know that she took advantage of all the learning opportunities that came her way!

I certainly learned ZIP codes in 1971. I learned the job of a secretary so I could understand when I had secretaries working for me. By the same token, if you start at the bottom, as MBA graduates who work for Frito-

Lay are required to do (this means driving a truck), you will always understand what those jobs are like and you will have more credibility because of it. In my career as a sales manager, it was to my advantage that I had done any job that my salesmen had to do. I knew the obstacles. I knew how to clean store shelves, take inventory, and negotiate with the department head.

The need to learn in unlikely places has been frustrating for you, as you did not understand why you had to take biology, or learn statistics. But you will profit because, maybe years from now, something will happen where that knowledge comes in handy. Why should a business major have to take biology? Whatever job you get, the chances are great that science knowledge will come in handy. In fact, more than 50 percent of the issues before the Supreme Court and Congress are in some way science related.

Comments from students that delight me sometimes are from people who don't really need to take my class. My recent graduate marketing class had two people who work in marketing for very large homebuilders. Because their undergraduate degrees are not in business, they have to take my class even if they work in marketing. I should not have worried, because they both told me they learned things in my class that helped them close more sales.

I teach a class in professional selling skills to undergraduates, as that is what I did for a living for 24 years before becoming a teacher. One of the students in my most recent class was not the kind of person who was interested in that subject, and her participation showed that to be the case. But, after the class, I got the following email from her:

> *"I just wanted to show my appreciation for the knowledge I have gained from this class. The positive outlook on life that I have gained is something so valuable that I will always try to carry it with me. This class has really taught me to look at life in a whole new perspective. For all that I thank you."*

Now that was worth it all to me!

"The Important thing is to not stop questioning"

—Albert Einstein

Abraham Lincoln, our sixteenth and perhaps our greatest president, was a man of decidedly modest roots. When campaigning for the Illinois legislature (which he lost),

> "*He passed reapers in a field, getting in the last of the wheat. The workmen had said they had little use for any candidate for either party, but would vote for any man who could do his share of the work; Lincoln promptly … borrowed a scythe, and led the crew on a full round of the field.*"[42]

As a future president, Lincoln had experienced all that the farmers he would represent were challenged by and it was one of his strongest attractions.

You have also been frustrated because you did not get that "magic" job right out of college, even though career counselors told you that you probably would not. After a year or so, things started to settle down, you identified (or you will identify) your real interests and things started to fall into place. I don't lie to my students (read: customers). Trust me on this one.

I am always amused at the "quick" fix advertising for diets, getting rich, etc. There is only one good way to lose weight and that is to use more calories than your body takes in. Investing is the same way. Many of my students tell me that they know a "quick" way to get rich. Then they find out that the "quick" way has some major risks associated with it. If you use this time to learn all you can about whatever you are doing, you will be glad you invested it and glad that you learned everything you did. Learning is never wasted. Whether you are learning ZIP codes or driving a truck, the experience is broadening your education and adding to your worth as a member of society. Many young people today expect to live the way their parents are living in middle age, without taking into consideration the fact that "to get from A to Z, you've got to go through all the letters of the alphabet."[43]

Former Secretary of State Colin Powell, while attending City College in New York, worked one summer as a porter at the Pepsi-Cola bottling plant in Long Island City. None of the white kids were interested, but the job paid $65 a week. When it came time for him to be hired for the next summer, Powell asked to be moved up to the bottling line. He had learned all about sweeping up broken bottles. He did not complain or belittle the experience, but he wanted to build on it. In his words: *"All work is honorable. Always do your best, because someone is watching."*[44] We can all learn from Secretary Powell's humility and grace. And from his persistence!

Everyone comes to college with a different "schema", or set of internal and external expectations. I had one student who was absolutely without focus when he first came into my office (in actuality, his advisor gave up and sent him to me). I made him take all the required courses, most of which did not interest him at all. Because I teach the senior capstone course for business majors, he had (emphasize the word *had*) to take my course. As happens with some of my students, the light finally went on! I am so happy to see this happen, especially when students have no focus for several years. He went to work for Enterprise Rent-a-Car right after graduation and I have been getting emails from him periodically. I got one the other day that supported my years of making him take courses because I knew he would learn something:

> *"I'm not the guy who came into your office so long ago with no focus or direction!!!. Thank you for helping me through all that and getting me on my way. I really do appreciate everything you have done for me."*

When Apple founder and CEO Steve Jobs gave the commencement address at Stanford in 2005, he spoke about how he just happened onto learning. The text of his speech is available on Stanford University's website. For reasons of copyright protection, I cannot publish it here, but his speech is often cited because the lessons he described are so useful:

- He spoke about *"connecting the dots."* Steve Jobs actually dropped out of college, but then dropped back in to take course he was interested in. Of course, this was not all romantic and he would probably not be able to do it today. He slept in the rooms of friends and returned soda bottles to earn money to buy food. One of the classes he "dropped in" on was a calligraphy class, where he learned about different type faces, a lesson that would come in extremely handy when he designed the Mac! Jobs was able to "connect the dots" of one learning incident to an opportunity that would affect millions of people.

- He spoke about *love and loss*, losing his job at Apple. Now, I'm sure it seems very strange that the creator of Apple could get fired, but it does happen. When there is a clash in vision or implementation at the top, the Board of Directors at some public companies makes changes at the helm.

  The reason that Jobs felt losing his job at Apple was a good thing (lemonade out of that lemon) was that he was now free to enter into creative ventures such as Pixar. When Apple bought another Jobs' venture, NeXT, Jobs returned and has been able to produce and innovate even more than the first time.

- The last area that Jobs talked about was *death*, his diagnosis of cancer and how it changed his life. Though he has recovered, the experience led him to ask of himself every day "If today were the last day of my life would I want to do what I am about to do today?" He suggested to his audience that they not waste even a single day living with other than their own goals.

- The end of the speech is *"Stay Hungry. Stay Foolish."*[45] This has all sorts of important lessons for you to remember as you face life's challenges and opportunity.

This is a real-life success story, but you see that it did not happen overnight and Steve Jobs had challenges that would derail people of lesser talent. But he looked for opportunities, opportunities to learn new things that would help him later, even if he could not articulate what they would be at the time.

Many of you will have children whose focus you will also need to shape. Take heart that they usually eventually realize that they learn something in lots of ways, as you did! That takes a lot of persistence on the part of the parents and teachers, but the result is greatness for many.

This past semester, I had a student who works for UPS. During a "penny war" to raise funds for a local charity, he brought his nine-year old son into my office with some pennies to show his son that giving to the community was important. That is modeling and it shows very fine parenting. After graduation, I got an email from him:

> *"Today while listening to La Verne's guest speaker from the Congo, the struggles of growing up in a war torn country and losing loved ones to AIDS and cancer, I realized right then that my journey was in no way any comparison to all that this man has lived. I was reminded by those few words you would say just before our next test, "There is nothing that bad that it should worry you," life goes on, we have someone to love and who loves us. You are right. I could not possibly compare my struggles to his, I am blessed with all that I have and all the opportunities that have been afforded to me."*

Edmund accepted this learning in an unlikely place, but he was able to put all the pieces together. His son is and will be the beneficiary as well.

The strategic management course at the University of La Verne is the last class many seniors take. It uses information from many of their previous classes, such as accounting and finance, classes they thought they were done with until they meet up with me! During the semester, I get lots of whining about how much information there is to absorb and how they can't wait to sell the book—until today! I got the following email from a former student and the message is exactly what I want for this chapter:

> *Janice,*
>
> *How are you doing? I'm doing pretty well. I started working about three weeks ago so it hasn't been too crazy yet. The reason why I'm writing you this e-mail is to thank you for what a great job you did teaching business seminar. I learned a great deal in your class, but never thought that it would apply to what I'm going to be doing in my career. As I began to study for the CPA exam I was surprised to see information dealing with strategic business management! I couldn't believe it. I never thought strate-*

gic business management would be on the CPA exam. I'm glad that I actually paid attention in your class because now the material is easy. So I just wanted to say thank you again. So if you have any accounting majors in your class and they plan on taking the CPA exam let them know that your class is actually on the exam so it might be wise for them to study the material now, so that they don't have to struggle with it later. Thank you and have a great day!

Jason Greenlee

Audit Staff
Audit Services
Deloitte & Touche LLP
Believe me, I read this email to my students every semester!

These last paragraphs remind me of the statement "Learning is not compulsory. Neither is survival." It is the same thing I sell my students when they complain about the cost of books, that education is expensive, but ignorance is far more expensive. The first statement above comes from W. Edwards Deming, the father of modern quality control (Total Quality Management, etc.). When he could not get people in the United States interested in his methods, he took them to Japan. From his successes there, our quality revolution was born. If you put learning in unlikely places to use, you will always be moving forward and always be benefiting from learning in unlikely places.

Integrity, Persistence and Discipline

13

The Real Gold is in Integrity and Trust, not in Gild-edged promises

Integrity is what happens when no one is watching. The person who leaves a note on a parked car he or she has hit or notifies the checker that they left something off the bill has an internal code of integrity. They do the right thing not because someone is watching, but because it is the right thing to do. People like this are valuable because they can be trusted.

There are three levels of moral development: pre-conventional, conventional, and principled. Pre-conventional people are concerned only with self. They evaluate actions based only on avoiding punishment, not on the validity of the action. Conventional behavior is characterized by what society expects, what others do. But principled behavior is characterized by an internal code of ethics. These are the people who leave that note on the parked car, the people who take their children down to the store after the child has stolen something in order to make the situation right. Principled people don't cheat when they have the opportunity. I once gave an exam where the person who copied them had inadvertently stapled the answer key to the exams. One of my students immediately came up to show me the key. That is principled behavior.

Textbooks will tell you that most people operate in conventional mode. Indeed, as young people go into business, the temptation to skirt ethics is mounting; a study at Duke University found that 56 percent of students pursuing a master's degree in business administration admitted to cheating.[46] This must stop or the consequences to our productivity and ability to compete in the world market will be disastrous. You can be different.

You can earn your success with principled behavior and the integrity so badly needed for us to set an example for the rest of the world.

Southwest Airlines is one of the most successful airlines in the United States, even though it was a mere startup not too many years ago. Herb Kelleher, the founder and retired chairman, had a very successful relationship with their union in part because of his integrity, the fact that he kept his word[47]. You did not need to get something in writing if Herb told you that it would happen. I hate to say that leaders like this are harder to find these days, but they are worth seeking out.

After the Malden Mills factory in Massachusetts was destroyed by fire, Aaron Fierstein did not accept the insurance company's suggestion to take their settlement check and retire. He did not decide to source textiles from the Far East, a far more sensible thing to do in his competitive business. Instead, Fierstein continued to pay each of his employees while the factory was being rebuilt. He insisted that his employees were the heart of Malden Mills. Without them, "there is no Malden Mills."[48] That is certainly integrity when no one is looking! Now, the accident happened in 1995 and Fierstein's generosity has not exactly been "happily ever after." The company is trying to climb its way out of bankruptcy, but Fierstein's gesture is no less admirable. When you do the right thing, many benefits occur.

The late J.C. Penny, as did many of our great entrepreneurs, worked at a grocery store as a boy. The grocer found a way to increase his income by mixing two grades of coffee together and selling the mixture for a higher price. Young Penny thought this practice so dishonest that he quit his job and made honesty and integrity the foundations of his many career decisions.[49]

Jon Huntsman is the founder and chairman of Huntsman Corporation, a billion-dollar petrochemical company based in Salt Lake City. In his career, Huntsman has given nearly fifty million dollars to charity. He feels that one's legacy is very important.

> *"A legacy centers around two areas. The first is character. A person's character—his ethics, integrity, and sense of loyalty, sense of graciousness—is as much a factor as financial dividends. The second is philanthropy. I'd say that 90 percent of wealthy people in America are not respected because they*

would rather make money than give it away. They've spent half their lives building great empires, but they don't have the joy of seeing the twinkle in somebody's eye when they give someone a scholarship or assist someone who is homeless. As a result, they lose fifty percent of the value of building a business. They're only half a person, half a legacy."[50]

> **"Character is like a tree and reputation like its shadow. The shadow is what we think of it; the tree is the real thing".**
>
> **—Abraham Lincoln**

I am not saying that you have to give all of your money away to have a strong legacy, or even give it all away to have integrity. But part of integrity is doing the right thing, working for the improvement of mankind.

eBay, the first consumer-to-consumer auction site, is a great success story and I believe it exemplifies the outcome of a business started with integrity, persistence and discipline. Now that they are a large company, they have many customers and stakeholders who want them to make changes or offer special discounts. In a review of their relationship with their customers and how Meg Whitman, their CEO, approaches these issues, Jonathan Tisch, CEO of Loews Hotels, lists these points:

1. *An atmosphere of trust doesn't just happen*
2. *Most people will do the right thing—and they deserve to be protected from doing the wrong thing.*
3. *Building Community sometimes means passing up easy profits.*
4. *Listen to community members, and then do the right thing.*[51]

In the business press, we see a number of articles about people and companies that "do well by doing good." By that I mean contributing to society in some way that also is good for investors, such as supporting local farmers or investing in environmental initiatives. It is a win-win situation.

Unlike employees of Al Dunlap, the famous "chain saw Al," who dismantled Scott Paper by selling it to Kimberly Clarke, where employees were secondary, companies that take care of their employees while expecting high productivity exhibit integrity. I urge you to seek out jobs with these companies and to eschew those where money is the carrot. Integrity lasts, but it only lasts if you keep watering it like the most precious flower in your garden.

"Doing good is more important than having a lot of fine things." In broadcaster Neil Cavuto's book, *More than Money*, he outlines struggles that many of his colleagues and acquaintances have gone through, from cancer to the death of loved ones. The following quote sums up his philosophy (and mine) quite well:

> *"Stocks are nice, but taking stock of what has real value is far more rewarding. Fancy homes are beautiful, but solid emotional foundations are more beautiful. Running a company is a worthy professional pursuit, but keeping good company is a worthier life-time goal.* "[52]

If you asked me who my heroes are, other than my parents, I would list near the top Barbara Jordan (1936-1996), the first black woman from the modern South to be elected to the House of Representatives, representing Houston, Texas. When she was first elected to the state senate, "They resented the hell out of a black woman showing up in the Texas Senate, they did everything they could to block her out."[53] Ms. Jordan knew she would be cloaked in the mantel of black militancy, given the times (1967), but she wanted them to know that she was not coming to carry the flag and sing "We Shall Overcome"; she was coming to work and to represent her constituency in Houston. In the United States House of Representatives, she did the same. She represented Houston, Texas, not ideals and issues that ran counter to the objectives of those who elected her to office. She "taught that there are seven core values that provide the framework for the American system of government: equality, liberty, freedom, justice, independence, respect for others, and opportunity."[54] I was fortunate enough to hear Barbara Jordan deliver one of the keynote addresses at Bill Clinton's 1992 nomination for President of the United States. Without a doubt, she was the finest public speaker I have ever heard. This was not only because she had an incredible and articulate speaking voice. It was because she truly believed and embraced everything she said and did. Even though my personal politics are very different from Barbara Jordan's, my respect for her integrity is not topped by any other person in the world. Pick these kinds of role models with whom to compare yourself.

You will find that excellent companies, the kind where you might want to spend your life, are run with integrity. "Astute business managers know that business success and ethical practices go hand in hand."[55] You will face ethical decisions many times in your career, and some of them will be hard to reconcile. It will not always be easy to "do the right thing." But the rewards of making it a habit include sleeping and living well. Thinking about what kind of person you want to face in the mirror each morning can go a long way toward maintaining behavior you are proud for others to associate with you.

Karl Eller, after whom the business school at the University of Arizona is named, has spent his career building companies in the outdoor advertising business. His most recent book, *Integrity is all You've Got*[56] really gets to the heart of why we need to live our lives with integrity. Here are the words that Eller wants to be remembered by:

> *Without integrity, motivation is dangerous; without motivation, capacity is impotent; without capacity, understanding is limited; without understanding, knowledge is meaningless; without knowledge, experience is blind.*
>
> *Experience is easy to provide and quickly put to use by people with the other qualities. Make absolute integrity the compass that guides you in everything you do. And surround yourself only with people of flawless integrity.*

Reproduced with permission

3M is one of the most admired companies in America and around the world. When a chemical they had used for forty years started showing up in blood drawn from people living all across the country, even though no evidence of danger to humans had occurred, they withdrew all products made with the chemical, including their popular Scotchgard® fabric protector. The Environmental Protection Agency applauded this move, because it was one that 3M did not have to make. They did it for the right reasons.[57] By the same token, as you read earlier, Johnson & Johnson withdraw all of the Tylenol on the market after five people were poisoned in Chicago in 1979. They did not have to do that either, as the crime only affected Chicago. This also cost them millions of dollars. But it was the right thing to do. We seem to read more about companies who spend the most time defending themselves than those who step up to the plate.

In management classes, we often talk about "walking the talk." Showing integrity rather than just talking about it builds trust in the workplace. Jack Welch, the retired longtime CEO of General Electric, writes a weekly column in *Business Week*, one of my most important educational tools. He and his wife answer questions from readers. Their August 14, 2006 column fits my point here:

> **Question: Is there a short answer for building trust in the workplace?**
>
> **Answer:**
>
> *"Yes, very short: Say what you mean and do what you say. Look, trust fritters and dies two ways. First, when people aren't candid with one another. When they sugarcoat tough messages. When they use jargon and baloney to purposely make matters obscure and themselves less accountable. The only way to get candor into an organization is for the bosses to identify it as a top value, consistently demonstrate it themselves, and reward those who follow their lead.*
>
> *The second trust killer is when people say one thing and do another. Again, bosses are the main culprits. They tell people to take risks but nail them when they fail. They endorse stretch budgets and invite people to dream big, and then punish them if the numbers fall short, even at the end of a decent year. They proclaim a commitment to customer service and let the factory ship less-than-perfect product to make the month's sales quota. Or worst of all, they espouse the company's values at the top of their lungs but keep and reward people who don't live according to those values simply because they make the numbers. The message that sends to the organization is: Nothing I say means anything. Don't trust me.*

Trust, ultimately, isn't very complicated. It's earned through words and actions instilled with integrity."[58] Reproduced with Permission

In all my years of sales and management, I can think of no better way to put this lesson than Welch does here.

Integrity, Persistence and Discipline

14

Keep Your Sense of Humor!!

In your college years, did you come across the little tidbit that smiling causes fewer wrinkles than frowning? That is not important to you now, but when you get to **MY** age, it will be the kind of thing that causes people to have Botox injections. It is much simpler to smile, and to laugh. Indeed, a sincere smile can do more to break tension and reduce walls when meeting new people than words can. My father gave me another excellent piece of advice when he told me to take my job seriously, but not to take myself too seriously. I enjoy making my classes fun (though my students don't think much of my joke-telling ability), and ask my students if they mind being teased. If they do, I find another victim. It is much more fun to learn in a pleasant atmosphere, and laughing helps make that happen.

In this atmosphere of political correctness, we are often afraid to offend someone. I try to set people at ease by laughing at my own physical handicap. I tell my students that I don't want to get emails the next day after some comment. But they still threaten, good-naturedly. Life is way too short to look for reasons to be offended.

Barbara Jordan said that a sense of humor is the most important trait a president can have. Think about the leaders you want to follow in your career and you will find that they have and use a keen sense of humor. If they are leaders you want to follow, they more than likely also exhibit a good share of integrity, persistence, and discipline.

Think of the classes where you learned the most. Was there an atmosphere of fun in the learning process? Of the jobs you have held so far, weren't the ones you looked most forward to the ones where there was a lot of smiling and laughing?

There has actually been a lot of research about the connection between exercise and the immune system, and now between laughter and health benefits. Dr. Lee Berk, of Loma Linda University, found that laughter increases the number of natural killer cells in cancer patients. These cells are the body's way of fighting tumors. So, just as orange juice is good for your health, so is making fun part of your life.

Dr. Bernie Siegel has also done a lot of research and publishing about mind body connection and spontaneous remissions in cancer patients.[59] Even the 1998 film *"Patch Adams"*, where Robin Williams played a doctor determined to bring laughter to his patients as a way to aid their healing, dramatized the importance of laughter in the most serious of conditions. It is likely that you will face difficult issues in your career and as your family grows. Remember to take the time to put laughter in your life.

Laughter is good for you; it produces endorphins that improve your mood. Your best memories will be filled with it!

Integrity, Persistence and Discipline

15

Believe in Yourself (Because I do)

You are all different, which makes you so interesting. You don't all have the same talents, but each of you is capable of creating a wonderful life for yourself and magnificently affecting the world at large. It does not have to be the invention of penicillin or the first hybrid car. Millions of people make a difference every day in small ways that balloon into enormous effects on society.

But you have to believe in yourself first. It isn't enough that I believe in my students, but I hope that helps. One of the most gratifying comments on one of my evaluations was "she also sees potential with the individual student and keeps them accountable for that potential achievement." Sometimes I am uncertain about my policy to not accept late work or to deduct points on papers for certain errors. But, if I didn't, those students would not be able to know that they learned well and learned from their mistakes. All those mistakes add to knowledge, and learning from them adds to my belief in my students, our future world leaders.

Imagine what would have happened if Rosa Parks had not refused to give up her seat to a white person that December day in 1955. Such an incredibly courageous act, refusing to go to the back of the bus because she knew her rights and she believed in them, was to change the course of history. I am quite certain that Rosa Parks possessed all the important traits discussed in this book.

Quinton Shields was one of those students who suffered through my goal setting lectures in pain. Although he had a wonderful personality, school was not his interest. So he failed most of his classes. Then we let him go to Barcelona for a semester, where he definitely did not use his talents (well, at least not his intellectual talents). But, I always knew that

Quinton did not appreciate and use his own ability. So I took a chance. I made him the coordinator of my General Motors Marketing Internship class, where he was responsible for leadership, planning, and a lot of goal setting. Quinton excelled! He went on to be hired by Pfizer as a sales representative for fifty thousand dollars, an excellent salary, and has continued to be promoted in that industry. Once Quinton realized that he could do things he never thought he could, that was his take-off point. But it took Quinton believing in himself, not just me believing in him, to make it happen.

I was excited to get a copy of our campus magazine recently and to read a story about Scott Lindeen, a former student who is currently playing for the Florida Marlins. As a Division 3 school, we don't have many baseball players go on to the majors, but everyone knew that Scott had the talent to do that. Though sidelined by tendonitis in 2004, he bounced back to be named Southern California Intercollegiate Athletic Conference Player of the Year. He said in the magazine that one of his favorite quotes is: "Start believing in yourself and others will believe in you. Prove those who believe in you right and those who doubt you wrong." While he was recovering from his injury, Scott used those words to keep focused.

Napoleon Hill, in *Think and Grow Rich*[60], said, "*Whatever you can conceive and believe, you can achieve.*" Immigrants to this country are four times more likely to become millionaires than native-born Americans. They have to believe in themselves to even make the leap to move here in the first place. You can instill that same burning passion in yourself.

Hill set out a self-confidence formula:

1. ***First, know that you have the ability to achieve your dreams;***
2. ***Second, realize that dominating thoughts will eventually reproduce themselves in physical action, and;***
3. ***Third, clearly write down the description of your chief goals in life.***

David Schwartz comments in *The Magic of Thinking Big* "*Not many people believe that they can move mountains. So, as a result, not many people do.*" [61]You were not yet born when President John F. Kennedy said we would walk on the moon before the end of the 1960s. But I clearly remember that July night in 1969 when we did!

In 1957, Homer Hickam wanted to build a rocket, a lofty task for a kid from Coalwood, West Virginia. Living in a company town, with a father who was superintendent of the coal mine, Homer had very little choice in occupations. But he believed in himself and he talked his friends into believing in his ideas. *October Sky* is the most important movie I have ever seen and I like to show it to my students as an example of goal setting and belief in an idea. Of course, Homer had a sponsor—his teacher, Miss Riley. She encouraged his desire to master the math and science necessary to complete his goal and she fought the disdain of the principal of Big Creek High School, who believed that all the boys would go on to be coal miners, not college students[62]. Homer and his friends went on to win the National Science Fair in Indianapolis, they all went to college, and Homer did go to work for NASA. They did all this because they believed in themselves.

Chester Carlson had to believe in himself because that's about all he had. After a miserable childhood, where he and his father actually lived in a chicken coop for a time, Carlson pursued his idea of xerography (now you know where Xerox came from). Unfortunately for Carlson, this idea was so obscure that the two dozen companies he offered it to expressed an "enthusiastic lack of interest" in what Fortune magazine would later describe as "the most successful product ever marketed in America."[63] When the Xerox machine was finally produced in 1960, Carlson's patent had expired. But he prevailed by "failing forward." He would try one method, find out it did not work, and try another. What seems so simple to us today in terms of making copies was indeed a very complicated process that required a lot of "failing forward" in cold rooms in Rochester, New York. Chester Carlson had to believe in himself to keep trying.

George Washington lost more battles than any general in modern history. He went to war against the greatest naval power of its time with a rag-tag army of ill-equipped and poorly trained soldiers. He had to believe in himself and in the capacity of the Colonies to win their way to independence because anyone looking at his resources would have told him there was no chance the Colonies could prevail. Lest you think that Washington had some special talents, remember that he had no more than an eighth grade education[64]. But he relied mightily on his advisors and even more mightily on his conviction that the American Revolution, which lasted eight years, was the right cause. In your life, you will come upon causes that are fraught with obstacles. Think of George Washington, believe in yourself, and press on! Remember not to listen too much to naysayers, who will be many the higher the goal. In his latest book, *Better than Good,* Zig Ziglar reminds us that *"In achieving your goals, it's not what others believe you can do; it's what you believe you can do"* (p.96).

Read good books and watch good movies, such as *October Sky* and *Seabiscuit,* which are truly great stories about people (and horses) who knew they could be winners. Read about Barbara Jordan. No one thought Barbara Jordan could practice law in Boston, much less become a congresswoman. But she did because she knew she could. I have some students with the talent of Barbara Jordan. All they need to do is believe in themselves.

I have had this saying on a card for many years and have no idea where it came from except Hallmark:

To be a star,
You must shine
Your own light
Follow your own path,
And don't worry
About the darkness
For that is when stars
Shine brightest!

Persistence means believing in yourself

16

Go after the A in Achievement, not the Grade

I said earlier that those who want extra credit are those who have not spent the time learning the material so they have to catch up. There is little doubt that those students who concentrated only on their grade did not learn much that they took with them or were able to use later. They spent most of their time asking me what was on the test. Education is expensive, but ignorance is far more expensive. Take from it all you can. I can tell you that one of the best courses I took in graduate school, an economics class, was one where I earned a failing grade. But I learned a lot!

A recent *Wall Street Journal* article bemoaned the current rash of tutoring and extra courses to raise grades. It also pointed out that many students are not interested in the material, just the grade. Today's young people think, "I'll learn it for the test, I'll do well on the test, and then I will flush it."[65] It should be obvious who loses here. It is mostly the person who paid for the education and did not get what he or she paid for because he or she did not see the value in it. But it is also the employer who expects that the person being hired really did learn those things. How much integrity, persistence and discipline exist in "learning for the test"? If you have to have surgery, do you care if the surgeon learned the material "for the test"? I hope so. For the same reason, employers hiring today's college graduates expect that they mastered the subjects so carefully listed on their resumes. Employers soon find out if the new hire studied only "for the test."

One of the courses I love to teach is "professional selling skills," drawing on my many years in sales and the many sales training seminars I have taken and conducted. I always start the class by suggesting *The Wall Street Journal* and *Business Week*, important tools in my continuous education. I also guarantee that the students will get their money's worth or I will pay for the subscription cost. Some students take advantage of the opportunity and they usually get a lot from the current articles in these publications. Luckily for me, no one has ever asked me to reimburse them the subscription cost! In the most recent professional selling skills course I taught, one of the students made it a point to send me a note about what the *Wall Street Journ*al has done for her:

> *Greetings Professor Dietz,*
>
> *"As this semester kicks off, and I do a little self-reflecting, I would just like to thank you for an amazing January class. I realized that I gained a lot of confidence in myself through taking your Professional Selling Skills and I catch myself giving my opinions more in my classes and thinking outside the box. I have begun to read as much as possible The Wall Street Journal and Business Week, and I get so proud to be able to discuss some of these topics with others. I am taking Principles of Marketing this semester and I am extremely excited that I am well prepared to participate and give a different insight to marketing. Through the class, my eyes were opened up wider to the business world, and how to be successful in life as well. From the bottom of my heart, I greatly appreciate you and your teaching style and I wish you the best of luck this semester."*

When you put extra effort into something for the pure value of it, the rewards are incredible!

When you go into your careers and have a chance to do something extra for someone, don't concentrate on what is in it for you, concentrate on what is in it for the organization and the customer. One of Zig Ziglar's most famous aphorisms is "*You can get have everything in life you want if you will just help enough other people get what they want.*" Think of the businesses, restaurants, and clothing stores where you spend the most money and are the most loyal. Doesn't Zig's theory hold true there?

Your professors and teachers made you do a lot of group projects because we know that your career will include a lot of collaboration, no matter what you do. You will be achieving goals for an entire group of people and an entire company, not just yourself. So the grade is immaterial. You will be judged on whether the objective was accomplished for the whole group. Achievement will take on a much more important meaning.

I had an interesting evaluation from a student who took my strategic management course last summer. This student, though a hard worker, seemed to concentrate only on the grade. When I corrected one of her assumptions on a test in a review of it in class, she said, "but you did not deduct points for it." I was shocked because she was not learning the material; she was accumulating points (learning for the test). When the evaluations came in, she pointed out that one of the important things she learned in the class was to concentrate on the material, not the grades. That was worth all my frustration in trying to get that message across to her!

Do an annual self-analysis and ask some of these questions:

1. *Have I attained my objectives for this year? (Answer this without blaming other people or things if you haven't. Then figure out how you can achieve them next year.)*

2. *Have I delivered more service than was expected of me?*

3. *If I had purchased my own services, would I be satisfied with the value? (This really causes you to think!)*

4. *Do I really know and study what it takes to be successful? What else do I need to do next year to ensure my success? How should I re-budget my time? How much harder should I work?*

This kind of analysis will help you face the absolute truth of your value and how to make sure that your own brand attains all of its potential.

Because many people like acronyms, here is an important one: ABL—Always Be Learning! Learn new things every day. Even though you have graduated, you are just beginning to experience all the wonderful opportunities to learn that will come your way. One of the secrets to longevity, and I know you are not thinking of that right now, is to keep learning. The more you stay engaged with opportunities to learn and to practice new material, the more you will stave off diseases such as Alzheimer's and mental slowdown.

Integrity, Persistence and Discipline

17

Set Stretch Goals

I have always been a goal-setter because I know that you need to know where you want to end up in everything you start. But don't set easy goals. If Roger Bannister, the first person to run the four-minute mile, had only set a goal that he knew he could reach, the record would not have been broken (as it has many times since).

You have to "see the winning." Selling is the highest paid profession in the world because it allows people to set and reach stretch goals. I spent thirteen years managing salespeople in the home center industry. The best made far more money than I did, and that was good, for them at least! They always set yearly goals for themselves that required a lot of effort. Easy goals were wasted on these stallions.

Study the goals that those you admire have set for themselves. Just as the key to success is to look at what failures do and refrain from doing it, the key is also to find out what "power performers" are doing and start doing it yourself![66] When you read that someone gets up at 4:30 am to work out before going to work, admire him or her instead of thinking "I would never do that." Setting goals, reaching some of them, and continuing to set them truly is the key to getting what you want.

When I used to train bank customer service agents to sell banking services (checking and savings accounts) in the mid-1970s, they complained about what would happen if they did not meet their goals. I told them that they would most certainly sell more with goals than without them. So the worst that can happen is you don't make your goal, this time. You just reset it or change it and go on! I was a jogger for fifteen years. I say jogger because I sense no one would have called me a "runner." When multiple sclerosis put an end to my jogging, I replaced the morning jogging with a goal to walk around the block several times. I can no longer do that either, so I pursue the goal of riding the exercise bike for thirty minutes at least three times a week. That works out well because I can use the time to read the *Harvard Business Review* and get two things done at once. Anyone you admire and want to emulate in your career sets goals. Think for a moment about people you admire and how they used goals to make the difference they have and presumably will continue to make. Write down the names of these people and make it a point to further study what makes them tick. You are likely to uncover some useful career information.

More than once in the past ten years, students who did not perform well told me "I am average, I am a laggard." Why they saw themselves that way I do not know, but no one is average unless he or she wants to be average. Everyone has within them the seeds of greatness, but they must want it. Anita Roddick, who founded Body Shop International, remembered that her mother told her to "be anything but mediocre." Now, founding an international cosmetics company is a pretty big way to avoid being "average," but the point is that you can reach your goals but you have to set them for yourself.

Those who set goals will accomplish far more in their lives than those who just go from day to day without objectives. If they write these goals down, they will accomplish even more. I used to tell people to put their goals in a scrapbook. One person put a picture of a Porsche in her scrapbook because she had a goal to purchase one by the time she was thirty-five. She did. There is also evidence suggesting that people with written goals accomplish far more than those without them.

I have been the beneficiary, through study, of the wisdom of two of industry's greatest leaders: Jack Welch at General Electric and Sam Walton of Wal-Mart. When Jack Welch became CEO of General Electric, he dictated that all GE's businesses *"Become #1 or #2 in every market they serve and revolutionize this company to have the speed and agility of a small enterprise."* If they weren't? (I was working for a division that wasn't) He divested them. It was a very clear goal and the performance of GE has benefited from it. Sam Walton also had a clear goal *"To make my little Newport store the best, most profitable variety store in Arkansas with five years."* The rest is history as Wal-Mart is the largest company in the world at this writing. These were compelling goals. You perhaps don't need such big goals right now, but the seeds of the goals that will propel your life into meeting your dreams must be there.

By the same token, not reaching your goals does not mean they are invalid. I was employed in the home center industry for seventeen years. I had a goal to become a vice-president by the time I turned forty. I did not make it. As a matter of fact, I never made it. But I had a glorious and full-filling career. Not reaching that particular goal did not make it invalid. It helped me to focus on achievement. So don't worry if you don't reach all of your goals. You will reach the ones that count. Just never stop setting them!

Earlier, I mentioned *October Sky*, a true story about 1957 Coalville, West Virginia. Four boys wanted to shoot off a rocket soon after the Soviets launched "Sputnik." But this was Coalville, a place that mined coal. That was their future; there was no doubt about it. College was not in the cards. But they had a goal and they had a teacher who wanted to help them. Even with the resistance of their parents and the school principal, they went on to win the National Science Fair in Indianapolis for their rocket design. They all went to college and one went to work for NASA. They had big goals, but they also needed big discipline and persistence to reach them.

Integrity, Persistence and Discipline

18

Never Give Up!!

President Calvin Coolidge wrote,

> *"Nothing in the world can take the place of persistence.*
>
> *Talent will not; nothing is more common than unsuccessful men with talent.*
>
> *Genius will not. Unrewarded genius is almost a proverb.*
>
> *Education will not. The world is full of educated derelicts.*
>
> *Persistence and determination alone are omnipotent.*
>
> *The slogan 'Press On' has solved and always will solve the problems of the human race."*[67]

Losing a sale is only one step closer to closing one. The law of statistical probability says that the more times you try, the more you will succeed. Look at baseball players. If a .300 batting average is good, that means that the ballplayer only got a hit thirty out of every one hundred times at bat. If I closed 30 sales out of every one hundred sales calls, I would be very happy, but I would still have been rejected seventy times—that means I would have had to "never give up" a lot!

Nothing great in the world has been achieved without a lot of failure, and of course, integrity, persistence and discipline. More than one hundred years ago, Asa Chandler, a young druggist, paid his entire savings of $500 for the formula of what was to become Coca-Cola, the world's most valuable brand. Asa Chandler did not know that then, but he knew the formula had potential. He had to believe in it and be rejected numerous times, but it was worth it in the long run.

No airline in history has survived the dramatic struggle that Southwest Airlines went through to get off the ground. Though you know Southwest as a major player in the commercial airline business and though we study their strategic advantages and policies in class, we do not talk too much about their start-up hardships. In fact, their fight to start this regional carrier had to go all the way to the Supreme Court because the competition fought so hard to keep them out. Herb Kelleher, Southwest's founder, kept saying, "*Gentlemen, let's go one more round with them.*"[68] If Kelleher had caved in every time the now defunct Braniff won a round, this fine example of marketing at its best would not be satisfying millions of customers and stockholders today.

In 1941, Winston Churchill was invited to Harrow School to speak to the young men at the same school where he, Winston Churchill, had repeated the eighth grade three times because he could not grasp the English language! He said later *"By being so long in the lowest form, I gained an immense advantage over the cleverer boys ... I got into my bones the essential structure of the normal British sentence."* "In October of 1941, at the height of the war, Harrow School invited him to return and speak to the young students. How eager they must have been as they waited with pencils poised. The greatest Englishman of all time was to talk to them and share the wisdom he'd gathered over an extraordinary lifetime. He stood up and looked out at the boys for a long, long time before he finally spoke. He must have been searching through the decades of memories to find just the right words for these future leaders. Finally he gave his entire speech in just a few words:

> ***"Never give in, never give in, never, never, never, never—in nothing, great or small, large or petty—never give in except to convictions of honor and good sense."***

And then he sat down."[69] Now, granted, Churchill was dealing with some very big goals, to protect the free world, but goals nonetheless!

I talk a lot about setting goals in every class. I hope that my students learn that you get further when you set them than when you don't. I hope they learn that breaking a desire to earn an "A" into the need to do ten percent better on each quiz or test really makes the goal achievable.

All great (and small) accomplishments start with goals. Would we have landed on the moon in 1969 if John F. Kennedy had not set that "stretch" goal in 1960? Now, **that** was a stretch goal! But they got there one step at a time, just like you will. If you set easy goals, you will miss the really great accomplishments of which you are capable.

A small book I read recently talks about "sticking to it." In it, Lee Colan reminds the reader that, "*When a bamboo seed is planted, it can take up to two years for a sprout to break through the earth. But once it does, it can grow over 100 feet in two weeks! This accurately describes the journey and benefits of building adherence.*"[70] I know that you are not very patient right now, but this example does a good job of showing how many accomplishments take patience and "sticking to it."

I have carried with me for many years a card that was left in my room at a hotel when I traveled for Johnson & Johnson to Bakersfield, California. Though the author is unknown, the sentiments are those that make the difference between those who dream and those who do:

If you think you are beaten, you are;
If you think you dare not, you don't;
If you'd like to win, but think you can't
It's almost a cinch you won't.
If you think you'll lose, you've lost.
For out in the world you find
Success begins with a fellow's will—
It's all in the state of mind.
If you think you are out-classes, you are;
You've got to think high to rise;
You've got to be sure of yourself before
You can ever win the prize.

Full many a race is lost—Ere ever a step is run;
And many a coward fails—Ere ever his work's begun.
Think big and your deeds will grow;
Think small and you'll fall behind;
Think that you can and you will—
It's all in the state of mind.
Life's battles don't always go to the stronger or faster man;
But soon or late the man who wins
Is the fellow who thinks he can.
Author Unknown

Persistence and believing in yourself are definitely all in the state of mind that you carry with you.

Here is an important story, to all of us, about persistence:

> *"At the age of seven, he was forced to work to support his family. At nine, his mother died. At twenty-two, he lost his job as a store clerk. At twenty-three, he went into debt (as partner in a small store), ran for the state legislature, and was promptly defeated. At twenty-six, his partner died, leaving him with a large debt. The next year he had a nervous breakdown.*
>
> *At twenty-nine he was defeated in his bid to become house speaker. Two years later he lost a bid for elector. By thirty-five, he had been defeated twice while running for Congress. At thirty-nine (after a brief term in Congress) he lost his re-election bid.*
>
> *At forty-one, his four-year-old son died. At forty-two, he was rejected as a prospective land officer. At forty-five, he ran for the senate and lost. At forty-seven, he lost the vice presidential nomination. At forty-nine, he ran for Senate again—and lost again …"*

Now, wouldn't you have given up after so many defeats? Who was this man who never seemed to learn and accept his defeats?

The man in question? Abraham Lincoln [71]

Integrity, Persistence and Discipline

19

Fail forward

David Cottrell says *"Success is ultimately realized by people who make more right choices … and recover quickly from their bad choices."*[72] Every failure is one step closer to any goal you set for yourself. The more hits you make, the more you will succeed. So it stands to reason that it takes plenty of false starts to get it right. As you saw from the previous chapter, Abraham Lincoln failed forward. He lost eight elections, went bankrupt, and failed forward until he became arguably the greatest president the United States has ever elected.

About 90 percent of new products fail. That means the entrepreneur must continue to try (and to fail) until the right thing comes along.

Thomas Edison is certainly one of our most gifted inventors, but even he failed forward:

Results? Why, man, I have gotten lots of results! If I find 10,000 ways something won't work, I haven't failed. I am not discouraged, because every wrong attempt discarded is often a step forward[73]

For many, the story of the invention of the Post-It® Note is well known, that 3M scientist Dr. Spencer Silver had given up on some glue he was working on because of an inability to stick strongly enough—until he needed something to hold his bookmark in place in his church hymnal. By 1990, this product was one of the five top-selling office supply products in America![74]

"I have missed more than 9,000 shots in my career. I have lost almost 300 games. On 26 occasions I have been entrusted to take the game winning shot ... and missed. I have failed over and over again in my life. And that is why I succeed"

—Michael Jordan

We all know Harland Sanders, the Colonel Sanders of Kentucky Fried Chicken (KFC) fame. Sanders failed forward as a streetcar conductor, railroad fireman, insurance salesman, and tire salesman until his secret formula for fried chicken gained local attention at a gas station in Corbin, Kentucky. All was well until a new highway bypassed his restaurant and he was broke again. So he began driving across the country, "spreading the gospel of Kentucky Fried Chicken."[75] Colonel Sanders failed forward right into millions!

Coach John Wooden led the UCLA Bruins to ten national championships. As you can imagine, that took great leadership, great discipline, and great teamwork. He says "A basketball team that won't risk mistakes will not outscore the opponent ... The team that makes the most mistakes usually wins."[76]

Did Microsoft ever have a failure? We tend to be caught up in the success of companies like Microsoft and overlook the failures they must have endured in the past. Did you know that both Windows 1.0 and 2.0 bombed as products? At one point in time, the Windows team was cut back to three people. But the team did not give up, and they failed forward into one of the most successful and innovative companies in history.[77]

If you have the chance to read the biography of Henry Ford, Winston Churchill, Andrew Carnegie, or Sam Walton, you will find that they failed forward into greatness on a number of levels, but they used the integrity, persistence and discipline that I am talking about here to achieve the greatness for which they are known.

Think back on admonitions from teachers not to read off the overhead when presenting in class, to speak distinctly, to proofread. Unless you have learned from the experience of doing it wrong the first time, you could be destined for mediocrity. There is an old adage that says, "Practice makes perfect." In actuality, practice does not make perfect. "Perfect" practice makes perfect. Any Olympic athlete will tell you that. Any opera singer will tell you that. Any musician will tell you that you must strike a lot of sour notes on your way to the kind of perfection that demonstrates success, but you must be practicing with perfection before you can attain it. And you can never stop practicing. It is like watering that plant that is you and your brand.

J.K. Rowling, the author of the Harry Potter books, is one of the richest women in the world, but her first Harry Potter book was not accepted for publication until a year after she finished it. She had to keep getting rejected, keep trying and keep "failing forward."

Joe Torre, who has led the New York Yankees to numerous World Series titles, says, "*You don't have to have a World Series ring to be a winner. A winner is somebody who goes out there every day and exhausts himself trying to get something accomplished.*"[78] It could be delivering the mail, teaching children, manufacturing a product. Winners are many and winning is an attitude. Each failure is one step closer to winning. Just ask Joe Torre!

"Success is the ability to go from one failure to another with no loss of enthusiasm."

—Sir Winston Churchill

"Our greatest glory is not in never failing, but in rising every time we fall."

—Nelson Mandela

One of the mantras that Zig Ziglar often uses in his public and published addresses is "failure is an event, not a person." What he means is that you must move on and keep your goals in front of you. You must not consider one failure as the defining description of your ability, character, or worthiness. I consider it very important to look beyond the grade a student earns on a particular assignment. Each of these is an event, not the student or even the sum total of that person. I want my students to enjoy and experience their education for its role in preparing them for the rest of a fantastic life, not for an "event" that will soon be forgotten.

"It's not what you look at that matters, it's what you see"

—Henry David Thoreau

Integrity, Persistence and Discipline

20

You don't Pay the Price for Success; You Pay the Price for Failure

As a college graduate, your income and success will dwarf that of your friends who did not take that route. Fifty percent of the jobs you will hold have not even been invented yet. If you are as lucky as I have been, and I expect you will be luckier, you can look back and realize that you enjoyed the process of moving through your career. There is no shortcut for success, though the lottery advertisements would lead you to believe otherwise. Las Vegas was not built on money people take out of those casinos. And if you think that a normal career won't make you rich, read *The Millionaire Next Door*[79] and you will see that slow and steady works just fine.

You pay a price if you pass up an opportunity. For instance, I frequently ask my students how many would leave and not return if I offered to give them a passing grade right then. The ones who raise their hands are willing to give up the learning for which they have already paid. In a ten-week class, students are paying about $150 a night. Education seems to be the only industry where customers don't want their money's worth. These students would rather go without the product they have purchased, learning that supports their dreams. I wonder how many of them would go to a surgeon who approached medical school that way.

The good news about this is that if you are one of those people who stay to wring all that you have paid for (and, hopefully, more) from an experience, you have catapulted yourself to the very top—those who enjoy the price of success and are rewarded many times over for it.

> "The quality of a person's life is in direct proportion to their commitment to excellence, regardless of their chosen field of endeavor."
>
> —Vince Lombardi

Ok, I have just used a quote from a famous football coach. I need to broaden the sports references. One of my students lent me a copy of *Wooden on Leadership*, by John Wooden, the legendary coach of the UCLA basketball team, which won 10 national championships under Wooden's leadership. I was just feeling guilty about my "no late assignments" policy when I read about Coach Wooden's very important methods of making sure that each member of his team was a winner, even down to their socks! When the team assembled for their first practice, Wooden discussed his few important rules:

Number one:	*Keep your fingernails trimmed.*
Number two:	*Keep your hair short.*
Number three:	*Keep your jersey tucked into your trunks at all times.*

Am I clear?"[80]

Perhaps now you can see what these things have to do with winning basketball games. If you hair is long, as you sweat during a game, you will invariably get that sweat on your hands and the ball will be slippery. Coach Wooden very carefully taught his players how to put on socks because that, too, mattered in the game. So did dress on the team bus, so did collegial behavior with their opponents, so did their academic performance.

In the end, it is the totality of your integrity, persistence and discipline by which you are judged. It isn't socks, or hair, or writing thank you notes alone that make the difference. It is the discipline to do each one with a plan for success, each one knowing it counts in the grand scheme just as much as the one slip of discipline that can set you back in your career for a long time.

If you start every day with a plan to give the most toward excellent performance, your record will even out in the long run. You will be enjoying the price of success and avoiding the price for failure.

Conclusion

By now, I hope you understand why I chose the theme of Integrity, Persistence, and Discipline for this book, In the twenty chapters you have just finished, I explained the importance of your personal brand, that persistence, "just showing up", can outflank a lot of other tactics, and discipline is required to make the others work well. During the past couple of years thinking about what I wanted to say, I kept coming back to the message I am sending. My first title was "Everything you needed to learn and were not ready to hear," but that title fails in the important message of the role that integrity, persistence and discipline play in living a fully fulfilled life. I truly believe that *"Nothing great or lasting in the world has been accomplished without them."* I gave examples of some pretty great accomplishments—the end of slavery, landing on the moon, inventing electricity, and the transistor. I hope you agree that the individuals responsible for these accomplishments would not have succeeded without the three ingredients on which I focused this book.

Remember that the top ten jobs in the year 2010 did not exist in 2004[81]. You will face many challenges on your road through the future, but these simple secrets (not so secret, are they?) will help you to make better decisions when faced with those challenges. You will know that the choices of how to act and how to respond to situations are easier when bounded by the principles outlined in this book. Successful companies, like Johnson & Johnson, have and continue to make use of integrity in mission, persistence in their goal to improve the lives of their customers, and discipline in reaching that goal.

Your degree confers upon you the responsibility to use it and to keep it current. Education is, indeed, expensive, but ignorance is far more costly. I hope that you will use many of the books referenced in this book to further explore your interests.

So, go into your lives with the knowledge that, no matter what your strengths, you can find happiness and you can make a difference when you live a life bounded by integrity, persistence, and discipline.

Congratulations! Come back and tell me how you are doing!

Integrity, Persistence and Discipline

References

Preface

[1] Drucker, Peter (1999). Managing Oneself. *Harvard Business Review*, Vol. 77, Iss.2,Mar/April, p.64.

Chapter 1

[2] Dvorak, Phred (2007). "M.B.A. Programs Hone 'soft skills'." *The Wall Street Journal*, 12 February, p. B3.

Chapter 2

[3] The Things They Do for Love (2004). *Harvard Business Review*, December.

[4] Brady, Diane (2005). "Yes, Winning is Still the Only Thing." *Business Week*, 21 August.

[5] Used with permission from Johnson and Johnson.

[6] Shula, Don and Ken Blanchard. *Everyone's a Coach*. Grand Rapids: Zondervan Publishing/Harper Collins, 1995.

[7] Plaske, Bill (2005). "He Can't Lose." *The Los Angeles Times*, 06 February

[8] Moore, Eva. The Story of George Washington Carver. New York: Scholastic Inc., 1971

[9] Riddles, Libby. *Race Across Alaska*. Mechanicsburg, PA*: Stackpole Books,* 1988.

[10] (2006). Enterprise Rent-a-Car: "A "Valuable" Foundation Supports its Continued Growth and Success." *Sold!* Illinois State University, spring.

[11] Tedlow, Richard S. *Giants of Enterprise.* New York: Harper Collins, 2001.

[12] Manilow, Barry. *Sweet Life: Adventures on the Way to Paradise.* McGraw-Hill, *1990*

[13] McCafferty, Dennis (2006). "Our 2006 Most Caring Athlete." *USA Weekend*, 01 October.

Chapter 3

[14] Ziglar, Zig . *See You at the Top*. Gretna, LA: Pelican Publishing, 1975.
[15] "Why Employees Don't Work to Full Capacity". www.Ezinearticles.com
[16] Ellis, Joseph . *His Excellency George Washington*. New York: Alfred A. Knopf, 2004, p.144.
[17] Ziglar, Zig . *See You at the Top*. Gretna, LA: Pelican Publishing, 1975, p.206.
[18] Thompson, Arthur A. *Wal-Mart Stores, Inc: A new set of challenges, in strategy: Winning in the Marketplace*, 2006, New York: McGraw-Hill, Second Edition, 2003,p.C-518.
[19] Lundin, Stephan, Harry Paul, and John Christensen. *Fish!* Hyperion Press, 2000.
[20] Reilly, David (2007). "How a Chastened KMPG got by a Tax-Shelter Crisis. *The Wall Street Journal*, 15 February, p.A1.

Chapter 4

[21] Weintraub, Aelene (2007). "Pushing Pills a Bit too Hard". *Business Week*, 26 February, p. 48.
[22] Carnegie, Dale. *How to Win Friends and Influence People*. New York: Simon and Shuster, Rev. 1981.

Chapter 5

[23] http://www.pbs.org/wgbh/pages/frontline/shows/navy/tailhook/invest.html
[24] Stauss, Bernd and Wolfgang Seidel. *Complaint Management*. Mason, Ohio:Thomson, 2004.

Chapter 6

[25] Sewer, Andy (2004). "Hot Starbucks to Go". *Fortune*, 26 January.

[26] Barnes, Nanette and Peter Burrows (2007). "Where Dell went Wrong", *Business Week*,16 February, p. 62.
[27] Ibid.
[28] Ziglar, Zig. *Better Than Good.* Brentwood, TN: Integrity Publishers, 2006, p.79.
[29] Riemer, Jack (2001). *The Houston Chronicle*, 10 February.
[30] Richard S. Tedlow. *Giants of Enterprise.* New York: Harper Collins, 2001.
[31] Eller, Karl. *Integrity is all You've Got.* New York: McGraw-Hill, 2005.

Chapter 7

[32] Fulghum, Robert. *Maybe (Maybe Not).* New York: Villard Books, 1993.
[33] Hill, Napoleon. *Think and Grow Rich.* New York: Ballantine Books, 1960.
[34] Dawson, Roger. *13 Secrets of Power Performance.* Englewood Cliffs, NJ: Prentice Hall, 1994.
[35] Beatty, Sally (2007). "A Hotel Family's Legacy". *The Wall Street Journal*, 09 March, p. W2.

Chapter 8

[36] http://homeport.usnaweb.org/parachute.html

Chapter 9

[37] Needleman, Sarah E. (2007). "If you want to Stand out, Join the Crowd". *The Wall Street Journal.* 14 August, p.B6.
[38] Gladwell, Malcolm. *The Tipping Point.* New York: Little, Brown and Company, 2000.
[39] Lublin, Joann S. (2006). Over Used Contacts Respond to Apologies, Rewards, and Updates. *The Wall Street Journal*, 4 January, p. B1.

Chapter 11

[40] Christensen, Clayton and Michael E. Raynor. *The Innovator's Solution.* Boston: Harvard Business School Press, 2003, p.75.

Chapter 12

[41] Flaccus, Gillian (2005). “O’Connor Talks About Family, Life Lessons.” *Inland Valley Daily Bulletin*, 28 October, p.A13.

[42] Hambly, Barbara. *The Emancipator’s Wife*. New York: Bantam Dell, 2005, p.342.

[43] Zaslow, Jeffrey (2004). “The Coddling Crisis: Why Americans Think Adulthood Begins at 26.” *The Wall Street Journal*, 6 January, p. D1.

[44] Powell, Colin. *My American Journey*. New York: Random House, 1995.

[45] http://news-service.stanford.edu/news/2005/june15/jobs-061505

[46] Gardner, Howard (2007)."The Ethical Mind." *Harvard Business Review*. March, Vol. 85, N.3

[47] Freiberg, Kevin and Jackie. *Nuts! Southwest Airline’s Crazy Recipe for Business and Personal Success.* Austin: Bard Press, 1996.

[48] Cavuto, Neil. *More than Money*. New York: Harper Collins, 2004.

[49] Cottrell, David. 12 *Choices…That Lead to Your Success.* Dallas: The CornerStone Leadership Institute, 2005.

[50] Bisoux, Tricia (2005). “Playing by the Rules.” *Biz Ed*, September/October, p.25.

[51] Tisch, Jonathan. *Chocolates on the Pillow Aren’t Enough*. Hoboken, New Jersey: John Wiley & Sons, Inc.2007,p.169.

[52] Cavuto, Neil. *More than Money*. New York: Harper Collins, 2004,p.277.

[53] Rogers, Mary Beth. *Barbara Jordan: American Hero*. New York: Bantam Books, 1998.

[54] Ibid

[55] Shula, Don and Ken Blanchard. *Everyone’s a Coach*. Grand Rapids: Zondervan Publishing House/Harper Collins, 1995.

[56] Eller, Karl *Integrity is all You’ve Got*. New York: Mc-Graw-Hill, 2004,p.90.

[57] Armstrong, Gary and Philip Kotler. *Marketing: An Introduction*. Upper Saddle River, New Jersey: Prentice Hall. 2005, p.576.

[58] Welch, Jack and Suzi (2006). “Ideas the Welch Way” *Business Week*, 14 August, p.88.

Chapter 15

[59] Siegal, Bernie S. *Peace, Love & Healing.* New York,: Harper & Row Publishers, 1989
[60] Hill, Napoleon. *Think and Grow Rich.* New York: Crest Books, Rev. 1960.
[61] Schwartz, David. *The Magic of Thinking Big.* New York: Prentice Hall, 1959, p.17.
[62] Hickam, Homer. *Rocket Boys.* New York: Delacorte Press, 1999.
[63] Owen, David. *Copies in Seconds.* New York: Simon and Schuster, 2004.
[64] Ellis, Joseph. *His Excellency George Washington.* New York: Alfred A. Knopf, 2004.

Chapter 16

[65] Gurdon, Megham (2006). Educational Supplements. *The Wall Street Journal*, p.W11.

Chapter 17

[66] Dawson, Roger. *13 Secrets of Power Performers.* Englewood Cliffs, NJ: Prentice Hall, 1994.

Chapter 18

[67] http://www.quotationspage.com/quote/2771.html
[68] Freiberg, Kevin and Jackie. *Nuts! Southwest Airlines' Crazy Recipe for Business and Personal Success.* Austin: Bard Press, 1996.
[69] Dawson, Roger. *13 Secrets of Power Performance.* Englewood Cliffs, NJ: Prentice Hall, 1994.
[70] Colan, Lee . "*Sticking to it*" Dallas: Cornerstone Leadership Institute, 2003.
[71] Stanton, Knofel. *Heaven Bound Living*, 1989,p.43-44.

Chapter 19

[72] Cottrell, David. *12 Choices....That Lead to Your Success.* Dallas: Cornerstone Leadership Institute, 2005.

[73] http://www.thomasedison.com/edquote.htm
[74] Ibid.
[75] Eller, Karl. *Integrity is all You've Got.* New York: McGraw-Hill, 2005
[76] Wooden, John and Steve Jamison. *Wooden on Leadership*. New York: McGraw-Hill, 2005, p.36
[77] Morse, Gardiner. (2007). "Set up to fail." Conversation with Economist Paul Ormerod on Strategy and Extinction. *The Harvard Business Review*, Vol. 85, No. 6, June.
[78] Torre, Joe (2006). "Joe Torre on Winning." *Business Week*, 21 August.

Chapter 20

[79] Stanley.Thomas J. and William Danko. *The Millionaire Next Door.* New York: Simon and Shuster, 1996.
[80] Wooden, John and Steve Jamison. *Wooden on Leadership*. New York: McGraw-Hill, 2005 p.149.
[81] http://www.glumbert.com/media/shift

About the Author

Dr. Janis Dietz is privileged to have enjoyed two very fulfilling careers. For twenty-four years, she held sales and sales management positions within the grocery and hardware/home center industries. She won the General Electric Sector Service Award in 1980, and worked as well for Johnson & Johnson and the Masco Corporation, managing sales territories for divisions which included Delta and Peerless Faucet.

A 1987 diagnosis of progressive multiple sclerosis prompted a career change for Dietz and she pursued further education to accommodate a less physically demanding employment. In 1995, Dietz was offered an opportunity to join the University of La Verne's College of Business, where she has taught marketing and strategic management for eleven years as well as advising their award-winning collegiate chapter of the American Marketing Association. She was awarded the 2006 award for Teaching Excellence at the University of La Verne. She has been published in the *Journal of Consumer Marketing*, the *Journal of the Academy of Business Administration*, *Marketing News*, and has presented her research at more than fifteen peer-reviewed conferences.

Janis Dietz is a native of Alexandria, Virginia. She holds a Bachelor of Arts degree in English Literature from the University of Rhode Island, an MBA from California Polytechnic University, Pomona and a Ph.D. from the Claremont Graduate University in Claremont, California.

http://faculty.ulv.edu/~dietzj

978-0-595-46926-0
0-595-46926-4

Printed in the United States
93932LV00004B/499-543/A